Love Letters to My Son

Foreword

D. JaSal Morris

Presented by

Ocir JaRon Black

Book Cover Art: Roy Beaman

Published by Write the Book Now, an imprint of Perfect Time SHP LLC.

ISBN: 978-1-7347783-9-7

Dedication
For the Love of All

The changing of time is important to us all.

Wondering and Waiting who will sit till the last day is called.

The sacrifices of the everyday man can be taken by the wind

Flourished and gone again.

Instead of listening and learning, they stayed outside, and we turned.

After all, losing one is what we will see, determining who is next

will be the worst for me.

After everything you lived for is taken from you,

Understanding what is left will build them up.

You will be missed, time and time again.

But not with a real understanding from where it all began.

- Ocir JaRon Black

In Memory of my "NaNa"

Sallie Mae Millner Morris Redd

October 22, 1931- July 3, 2017

You are FOREVER in My Space.

My world will never be the same.

In Memory of my Amazing Godmother and Friend

Robin LaVonda Curtis

May 9, 1973- May 14, 2020

Your love for us can never be measured.

Thank you for ALWAYS being there for us.

TABLE OF CONTENTS

Acknowledgments

Rico Black

Thank you Dad for ALWAYS helping me

to believe in myself. You are my foundation.

Zyon Black

Thank you for keeping me in my right mind

and always keeping me calm. Together, we will

change the world. #seeOzRun

Roy Beaman

Thank you for taking my vision and

creating a masterpiece.

Evan Martin

Thank you for capturing the personality

in every shot.

Dr. Sharon H. Porter

Thank you for believing in my dream and making it a reality.

I am forever grateful.

Foreword

A bond between a mother and a son is special. A mother knows she is to provide love and guidance at all times whether it is wanted or not. My mother never stopped and as I got older, I always got the guidance through love in cards or letters. Mom died three years ago. Recently, I was going through some papers and cards and came across some of the letters she sent me. Some made me smile and brought a tear to my eye. These are special as they let me know in her absence what I meant to her. Unfortunately, I also had the attitude I had to some of what she wrote. As an African American male, some of her guidance I better understand now, than I did when she wrote to me. One thing about a letter versus a conversation, you can always read a letter again as one may hear "Go read that letter I sent you and act as you read it".

I often wonder what she would write concerning what is happening today. The mothers featured come from different generations, socioeconomic, life experiences, and levels of faith. The letters from these mothers tell their sons how special they are and will be an inspiration to all who read them.

Derrick JaSal Morris
Oldest Son of Sallie Morris-Redd

Introduction

Who am I? A question that has more value to it than any other question in the whole world. A question that I have been asking myself all my life. The one question that my brain refuses to answer because the reaction will be far more upsetting than appeasing. The only question that could make or break your day. But, it is the only question that I am most confident about answering.

Learning from what my parents have taught me, I am an African American male that was born into this world to do incredible things. Everything from the top of my head to my pinky toe is special and no one in the world can take that away from me. But, learning from what the United States have taught me, year after year is that, I am an African American male, that will commit a crime, I am in a gang, I do drugs, I want to throw away my life, I want to steal any and everything I see, I don't have a dad and my mother is the only person that takes care of me. My only role models are professional sports players and I don't want to be successful in life. The history of my people doesn't matter because the only thing we care about as a nation is "White Power". It is very easy to have that implanted in your brain because that is what you have been taught all of your life or that is what we see on television. The world doesn't want black people to be successful. They just want us to do the lowest jobs possible: But that's not what my parents have taught me.

My mother has always been the person who helped me the most when it comes to School and Education. Back in 6th grade, she told me about a school that was in Forsyth County and she wanted me to look into the school and see if I wanted to apply. The name of the school is Early College of Forsyth. I immediately fell in love with the school and when people would ask me what high school I was going to, I would tell them "The Early College". Fast forward four years. I am currently a Sophomore at the Early College and one thing that I learned Freshman year is that there aren't a lot of Black Males at my school. This has nothing to do with Early College and how they accept people. This is because a lot of Black males don't want to go through an interview and have to take a test just to be accepted or declined from the school. Because of that, I am often the only African-American male in my classes, High School and College. The most important thing that I tell myself is "I belong in this class, I am just as smart as everyone else (Student wise) and I want my talents to show louder than my skin color is."

So, for the people who want to know Who am I? Here it is: I am an African-American Male who attends school every day, works hard and pays attention, I have never stolen or taken anything in my life and don't plan to. Both of my parents live in the same house and are very active in my life. I've never committed a crime and never plan to. I am a Student-Athlete who's role model isn't a professional athlete, he is a real life leader, my uncle, Derrick JaSal Morris because he beat the odds to become successful. At the end of the day, people will always view me as a black male, but I want them to view me as a black male in power.

How to Counter Low Expectations

By Ruthmarie B. Mitchell

My Baby Boy- A prophetic word for you

My first born, my son, this world is not ready to witness the barricades that you will knock down with ease. The limitless success you will achieve. You will be a force to be reckoned with. Not because you are the descendant of kings but because you will have high expectations for yourself and those who surround you. You will be called "different". You will not fit into the mold that has been carefully orchestrated for you and those who look like you. Society will be forced to recognize you apart from your hue.

I will teach you how to focus on yourself as an individual, while maintaining pride in your heritage, never losing your identity. You will be the very best that you can be, attributing everything to what the Lord has already planned for your life.

You will understand how the media is designed to impress upon you an image of Blackness that does not include education, family, or success. You will experience moments of disrespect and discrimination, both overt and covert. But you will recognize the system that is. You will rise above the line and crush all ceilings, not just a few.

You will have a plan, one that takes you along the path already established in Jeremiah 29:11. Son, you will be the very best that you can be because they said you cannot. You will dust yourself off and shake all negative vibes. You will fuel your soul and ambition with each No or Maybe. You will be a change agent within your own circle. You will measure yourself against yourself and only seek God for approval. You will have the faith of a mustard seed in due season, in every season. You will make a mockery of the system designed for you to fail. You are greater than the expectations of many.

As you reach each goal, each success, you will crave your next victory. Make no excuses and forge ahead. Strive to have your name listed in the books of historical record breakers. Hold your head high in the face of your enemies and trust that you wear the armor of God. Regardless of what waits ahead, you are unstoppable. You will be a Chief among men and respected for the path you create for others like you to follow.

Born to rise above the rim. Your level of excellence, your drive, and commitment to your purpose will rebel against all negative expectations. They will be forced to recognize and honor you for your outstanding achievement. And although they will call you "different", you will know that your difference does not matter.

Mommy

A Mother's Love

True love shows the truth in people.

Only the real ones would know,

Understanding the love of the mother

Is on the only beginning of the show.

Believing what you can't see is hard

But loving what you know real change your life

The Black mom is strong, She cares and protects her family.

The Black mom is wise, Sharing her knowledge everywhere she goes.

The Black mom is fierce, Able to stand up in what she really believes in.

The Black mom is understanding, Helps push her children to the best ability they can be.

The Black mom is black, not allowing her race to stop her from fighting the good fight.

Ocir JaRon Black

Them Boys of Mine

By LaShonda Scott Douglas

"Them Boys of Mine"

You will remember me if I tell you. Even if I write. Words written on paper may fade, but me telling you I love you, will be forever written upon the table of your hearts. 2 Timothy 3:14-15 14: But as for you, continue in what you have learned and have become convinced of, because you know those from whom you learned it, 15: and how from infancy you have known the Holy Scriptures, which are able to make you wise for salvation through faith in Christ Jesus.

Regardless of the upbringing we all may have experienced, those lessons learned will become a part of the foundation in which we all will build upon. To my kings, my sons, those boys of mine. My love for you is a forever kind of love. The wisdom shared with you as becoming men, I pray you both keep near and dear to your hearts, until it's no longer needed. The cord attached was not the connection that kept us close, it was the love. You two boys are the part of me that I'm able to see only through you, that I consider good. True wisdom comes from Christ Jesus, and the ones He so purposely chose to use to share with us on this journey. A journey we call life. As I write, think, and direct my heart's voice towards the significance of my sons' lives, it moves me to tears. Them boys of mine, can make me cry, laugh, smile, and even put me into a fit of rage, in a matter of seconds. But as gifts, they were given to me, and forever they are mine. Unconditionally you taught me to love, in such a manner in which no one breathing could ever comprehend. From selfish to selfless, have your presence shown me myself.

As I love, as deeply as any mother can express to their sons, never forget who you are, and whose you are. The love that God has for you, is truly an everlasting kind of love. He loved you both enough to allow you to be here to share your lives with the world. With an intentionally planned future, and hope for everything you may desire, have faith to know it's all just a prayer away. Recognize your worth, walk in your calling, be mindful of the gifts, and understand the price that was paid for your souls. You are worthy of every good thing you're able to dream of, or speak aloud for. Learn from that lesson that may have saved your life. And especially the ones that will. The one that doesn't feel so good, or maybe not even fair. God loves you so much and if you stop fighting, and allow Him to do it for you, you'll be thankful for the time and energy you have saved. I've been given the honor and privilege to be called "Ma, Mama, Madre, Mamaaa, and Mother"(when it's a request that usually follows!) Entrusted with presents, that would continue to give to us, and to the world around them. Servants are what we are to God, and His people are to whom He expects us to serve. Never think that you're too good to be able to reach down and pick up another brother. The same compassion used to keep your relationship with the Lord, is the same that you will need to show to others. No, it will never matter concerning whatever name, title, or position you may have. The personality and respect you show the world, will only be illustrated when following the Plan laid before you. Learn and understand those things that you've been given, and be able to discern how much is required to get it done. There will never be a mistake, shortcoming, fault, or error made that He won't forgive you and deliver you from. If you ask Him sincerely to help you. He loves you not only that much, so much more.

To my eldest, my first true love. From the moment I heard of your soon arrival into my future, I held you closest in my heart. God knew what you needed, and how I would need you even more. Your birth meant greatness to me. Your name means one willing to learn. And oh how you have lived up to your name my son. The harder way is how you have gained the most wisdom. Your mental stamina and desire to help others, are gifts only from God. I laugh at every opportunity you take to remind me of pulling my "Mama Card!" Remember who can only pull the "Mama Card", Yes, ME! The strength you have been given will carry a lot of weight, but never carry what God is trying to hold and carry for you. I knew I had someone great, when only I was willing to fight for even your unborn life, before even seeing your little face. You are, and will always be loved and even more, you will ALWAYS be mine. Son, you were my first true love, my motivation for life, and a reflection of unspeakable joy that still can make me smile. Thank you, baby.

To my protector, my baby, the youngest with the oldest soul. You were not a surprise to us, but a true miracle and fighter since day one. The moment I shared with your Daddy we were expecting you, he just knew in his heart he had another son on the way. Little did he know he would get to see himself, hear himself and give instructions to one who remembers and honor his every word. You have brought so much joy and laughter into my life while watching you grow by leaps and bounds toward the man God is creating you to be. Your life has in turn given me life. I have poured out, and drawn on that strength more than you would ever know. I love the mind and heart of compassion you have been given. Your love for God, and deep conviction for how you see the world around you, will cause this earth to shift on its axis because you refuse to give up on your beliefs. I LOVE THAT! But remember all debates stop where? Yes, with Mama! The wisdom that you walk in, your understanding of God's Word, will keep you, carry you, and grow you to be the person you so desire in your heart to be. As for your zealous spirit, never lose it. And if you happen to, look up and you'll find it again.

At the end of every day, I pray you both can look in the mirror and see the gifts you are to the world in which you live. One of the most important decisions in life you must make as men, as leaders, as children of God, is whether you both will leave your mark on the world, or allow the world to leave its mark on you. Life was not only given to you to simply wake up every day and hope something happens. Get up and make it happen. Faith without works is dead. Life, jobs, careers, titles, or any type of employment will never measure up to who you truly are and what you have been called to do. Life has a way of simply happening to all of us. But it's our choice as to what we accept and deem true. Brilliant are the minds you have received, with responsibility attached to it. Changes you see that need to be made, make them in you, so others can follow. We are in the world, not of the world. Now change it for the good.

Proverbs 1:8   Hear, my son, your father's instruction And do not forsake your mother's teaching; Experiences as becoming a mother has opened my eyes to seeing life from a totally different perspective. From the wife, mother, and planning a promising future with your father, to tearing up plans that were forever changed, when God decided it was time for him to come home. He loved, cared for, taught, but most importantly, lived the life he preached in front of you. Izaric, days before making his transition to Glory, he sat you down and gave you specific instructions on what to do if he didn't make it home. Being attentive, yet still wondering why he was talking to you like that. I will forever believe he knew, he just didn't know when, but he knew. In life, sometimes the details can be a determining factor of success or failure. From the moment the decision was made to let go, memories are all we have left. God's Plan is Perfect, even when we don't understand. Being a young mother never came with an instructional manual, especially after braving the storms of life alone. Or when I felt like I was alone, but God was and will always be there.

Life can be so challenging at times. Trying to decide whether to do right or to do wrong. Making up your mind if I'm going to live the right way, or live the way I want to live. Looking at the world around you, and seeing most people's moral compass is way off kilter, questioning yourself, do I enter the narrow gate, or follow the crowd through the road that is broad? Choices will forever be up to you to decide but choose wisely with the consequences whether good or bad. My sons, let me encourage you. One of the biggest challenges you may face is having the ability to live in and be forgiving, in a not so forgiving world. Tests will come, but they will only come to make you stronger. Even when you are at your weakest, speak strength to yourself. Trust God. Since birth, you have everything in you to make it. You boys will overcome any and everything you put your mind, heart and hands to do. When you thought I was being hard on you, fussing over what you wouldn't do, when I knew you could do it, will be revealed to you by and by. Remember we are all relational beings and those near and dearest to us will cause us to know, grow, and ultimately teach us how to sow into the lives of others. Salvation will forever be the most important and meaningful relationship we all will have encountered with Jesus. Whatever may come and go in life, please allow your personal and intimate relationships with God to grow you boys, into the men you were predestined to be. Our faith has already been tested by so many years of uncertainty, pain, hurt, and loss. Still, the fact remains, and I'm so certain of it. Being an overcomer to the things the enemy thought was going to destroy you, will make you go that much harder to make him out of the liar he will forever be. Never do you have to prove anything to any man, or woman, about who you are. Whenever you make it over, use wisdom, and remember to always go back to get someone who can't find their way.

After having an enlightening conversation with a young lady concerning how God has given me the strength to continue raising my children by myself, I came to a breath-taking realization. I have never, nor will I ever be a man. I will never again say, or believe another saying "I have to now be both Mama and Daddy because God allowed My Love to finally rest. Don't you ever believe the lie that a mother can ever take the place of his father. Or vice versa. There is such an obvious distinction in the role of a mother and father and I believe intentionally created that way. You are not going to be able to do but what God allows you the ability to do. Your growth as becoming the young men your father and I so prayed for you to become, has already been taught to you, by your father. He couldn't leave you until he did what he was created to do. For that, I am eternally grateful and honored to have been a part of the Plan. Live in your own Truth, which was, is, and will always be the Word of God. Good health, abundant wealth, and joy for your soul, is yours for the asking. Please always take note of your own well- being and take good care of yourself, first spiritually, physically, and even emotionally. Laugh often, talk when you need to, be quiet if it is not worth the argument, dance every chance you get! Just let the music play!. I know who your Daddy was, and how being competitive is simply a part of who you are as well. It's just how you were built. In life just know that your greatest opposition will never be the next man, it will be yourself. No one can ever be you, so if they can't be you, they can never be a better you. Focusing on yourself to become the men you desire your sons to grow to be, will cause you to evolve to become him. Sharing life with "them boys of mine", has been one of my greatest personal accomplishments ever. They have helped me see myself when I wasn't looking at the whole mirror. Please listen to your children even closer than I was able too. Teach them to love, respect and cherish each other. Remember, they will be yours. They will have a lot to say.

Ephesians 6: 1-4 1) Children, obey your parents in the Lord, for this is right. 2) "Honor your father and mother"-which is the first commandment with a promise- 3) "so that it may go well with you and that you may enjoy a long life on the earth." A mother's love for her sons is truly strength beyond measure. With the same arms we swung them around with as a child, will be the same arms, used to help hold us up when we may fall as time waits for none of us. Being obedient will bring about bountiful blessings, including the chance of long life. Idris and Izaric, it is such an honor, privilege, and blessing to be called your mother. But even more to be able to call you both my handsome, loving and intelligent kings, my sons. Quitting is never an option going this way, but finding another way is. The young men you are, will not compare to the Glory that will be revealed growing into the awesome Men of God you will become. Years of lessons, love, successes, and failures are why everything you touch, God will bless, You have made me so Godly proud, and I will forever love and thank God for your lives. Do Work.

Love Always,

Mama

The Play Book

By T.C. Evans

To My Dearest Son,

I hope this message finds you well and you are as excited to discover this message as I am eager to write it to you. Over your lifetime there have been so many memories we have shared and during those times I wish I had taken better notes and captured all of your reactions and milestones. I wish I would have written down all of my thoughts and stories which were sparked by every little thing you would do or say. You have been such an amazing addition to my life as my child. I would never change anything about you. Son, I feel and believe my overall duty as your mother is to make sure you are ready for this ever changing and sometimes unforgiving world and for you to become a great person possessing great qualities to pass down to who comes next. I hope your reading this serves as a compass of sorts or at least a basic understanding of my unconditional love throughout your lifetime. May you always be blessed to love and be loved, search for and find wisdom, gain loads of knowledge, and I pray you will know when to use every tool you have gained when you need them the most. Enjoy this journey.

I will have to start with the earliest memory I can recall during my imaginary play moments as a little girl growing up in a small southern town. In those moments, I always imagined myself having a family with children running around full of laughter, love, and closeness. Thinking of my children running through the house, making every moment joyous was how I pictured my future. Our family has always been my safe spot. I truly remember envisioning you, my son, before I learned how to care for myself independently. Before I could even entertain answers to questions of who I was as a person, who I was called to be, or if I would ever be successful at any of the things I set goals for or dreamed to do, "you" my son, were always one certain person I always wanted. So, I am convinced this is where my love for you was initially planted. I had no idea what the real you would sprout to be in years ahead, needless to say, I could not have picked a more perfect son for me than you.

During the time you were physically growing in my tummy our connection developed too and I wanted to do my best to give you the world. My love grew deep roots, making it impossible to be cut away. In fulfilling my duty as a mother, I want to be a model for you. Not quite the runway, fashion, or magazine type models who are most popular, but I want to show you all the lessons I've learned, mistakes I've made, and how this whole thing called "life" all works.

Through my life experiences, I realized my "grand idea" of wanting to make everything right and good for you may not be the best for you. However truth be told, I do not have all the answers. In the meantime, we will continue to figure it out together. We will continue to do what I know how to do such as play, spend quality time, and share. I can show you how to play, how to build with Legos, how to share your emotions, and be comfortable having silly conversations every now and again. Laughter is good for the soul.

Ensuring you had all the material toys or things was a phase. Providing you with all the resources you need to live and get through life has become my ultimate focus. In society, things or material toys, technology, games mean so much more when you work hard for them. Earning what you need and want carries more significance. Saying "no" to you when you were younger was very devastating to you then. I do not know if you remember, but you just could not (or maybe would not) understand why. I have to say "no" and enforce rules because not understanding right from wrong as well as respect for others and hard work now; will prove to be even more devastating for your future self. I do not and will not always get it right, but I hope you understand tough love is most certainly a necessity that will continue to show up when it is needed. Son, I want you to know that through living, I have learned *nothing is given to you without some sort of cost*; whether monetary or in deeds, or in future loyalty. Looking at the times, it is proving more than ever you will have to work for what you want in life and where you want to be in life. I wish I could say this world is nice, easy, or even great, but that is not always true. Be brave because not all times will be great, happy, or triumphant. There will be times when you will fall, fail, slip, and maybe you will feel like turning around. This is when you remember me coming to your side and hugging you to shield you from all the harm of the world.

I have watched you grow over the years, despite it being the early years of your life, you have always liked to build. Your life process may look totally different from my own or any of your peers. You will be on unequal playing grounds and it will not be fair. It may be simple, but it may also be rocky and all uphill. Never quit! Psalms 23: 5 says, "You prepare a table before me in the presence of my enemies..." At times when there is not yet a table, building the table may be your only option. I want you to know you have permission and you can! Do not be afraid to build what you need with your own hands. Build the table and it will be prepared for you. I love to see you work hard to use your creativity. Stay "create-full"! (A word you used when you were young to praise yourself for something you made.) Son, you will always find your way.

Another dimension of being your mother who loves you is caring for your well-being and protection. Since you have been here on this earth, most times I find myself fussing certain statements to keep you safe. You have heard me say: "Stop that!", "Why are you jumping?", "Get-off-of-your-head!", "Slow down." Another lesson to gain from me as I try to protect you is arming you with the understanding: *Son, you are in charge of you!* I also tell you, *"only you can control you."* I want to teach you and guide you to know yes, you are in charge of yourself, however, what you choose to do with that charge can be the difference in a moment or time of celebration or a consequential time of discipline.

There are people who will come into your life and there will be some who will not stay. It is important for you to put in the work on increasing and managing your own mental health: your anger, your temper, your patience. People will love you, like you, and maybe despise you, and there are also those whose intentions are not aligned for your overall good. Remember that table I discussed earlier? It said, "..in the presence of my enemies." Son, a lesson to understand is everyone is not good for you. It is true, everyone will not be your enemy, some will be friends, and some may even be family members. Sometimes you can control it and sometimes you cannot; you will not even see it coming all the time. Therefore, only you can control you, and if you need help with how- ask for help.

My love for you, you see, was established before you even were born--insert your initials here--and now you are here and I have had the great opportunity to share several years with you, my love for you has grown exponentially. I never could have imagined the series of events that would lead to what has proven to be some of the most difficult transitions in our lives. One of these transitions includes separation. The parting of the two people you have known all of your life. I find separation one of the most difficult subjects to discuss because you are still so young and the nuances of adult decisions are not your burden to bear. To be honest, when we are apart from each other, this is one of the heaviest loads to carry. Throughout this time, I still want you to be free to play and be silly with friends all while having the security of knowing you are protected and cared for as well as safe and loved. I know things have changed now and that is simply a fact. In all this, I want to be your shield and buffer. I will willingly take hits for you if it means you will have an easier time. For you, I will stand in all the elements to shield you from any anguish this transition may cause you because I love you.

You are young and this journey is just beginning, as I imagine you will feel it impact you throughout your lifetime. So I understand, shielding you long term may not be the best way if it keeps both sides of the truth from you. I realize I need to give you what you need on your level to be able to cope and adjust just like myself; we are both adjusting. So, I shield you in other ways like being intentional about how I speak and be sure to respond with respect in terms of all parental figures involved. In addition to being careful as to what details I speak about because you do not deserve to get "caught in the crossfire" of adult situations. Separating had nothing to do with you. It is not your fault, I know it "sucks" because we spend so much time apart. You are welcome to share your feelings of frustration, anger, sadness, and whatever you feel. Your social and emotional well-being is just as important to me as your physical well-being. I did not plan this or imagine this when I was imagining you and my family as a little girl; this was not my goal. No matter what I am here for you. No matter when I am here for you. No matter how I will get to you. I will never be separate from you.

My intent is to make you feel safe, loved, protected, and happy. It does get a little complicated when transitioning between two households becomes the new normal. I get worried because, yes I made a decision that has the potential to change your life. Yet, I had to realize and repeat to myself because there will be more times when a decision needs to be made that may change your life, but instead, it may be about " to ride the bus or not to ride the bus" or to play soccer or pick an instrument. Both will impact your life in different ways. Overall my vision and desire for you is to know and see what happiness is like in real life for you and others around you. I want to give you the best parts of myself and I needed a change for that to occur. Despite the road ahead, part of me knows I can give you a happier and more present version of the Mommy you need. I pray that one day you can understand-I want the best for you. My prayer is also that you may one day understand the separation of your parents for yourself to a point that you can find your own peace about it while believing and knowing both of your parents love YOU tremendously and it is everlasting.

Son, I want you to be brave enough to try things you like and find your interests, go places you've never been, continue to set goals and dream as big as you imagine. I hope you never place yourself in a box, never settle, never dumb yourself down. You don't have to fit in, just always be you! *"Always believe in YOU"*. Despite this, it is important to remember who you are and you are enough. You can always improve yourself, mentally, spiritually, and physically. Empathy, sympathy, helping others, responsibility, respect, sincerity, and apologies can go a long way. Yet do NOT change for someone else. Change for you! My hope for you is that you remain confident in yourself. Please know and understand the great person you have grown into; you have greatness in you. Always be open to learn and learn from everyone, but in all of your gaining of information, be you! You are beautifully (handsomely) and wonderfully made.

Be strong, big boy, it's going to be alright. I, as your mother, will always want to pick you up, dust you off and put the "magic" and a band aid on it and make it all better. Yet, I remember my mother's wings cannot extend to all areas or places, and some things you will face on your own. The most reassuring thing I know is that you will be amazing on the other side. Remember every fall, you can get up; every failure you can turn into a success. You can recover and turn it around. The goal is to keep moving. There is a next step, next project, next goal, or the next idea because you, my son, are infinitely great!

I see your potential even at an early age. You have ambition and can be a hard worker, but you also have a hard head. There will be challenges along the way. Many times the biggest challenge I have faced was myself. I was my worst critic and never allowed myself time to enjoy many things in life. So Son, love yourself enough to let yourself live. One of the greatest encouragements I've lived by throughout my life has been: "Not that I am speaking of being in need, for I have learned in whatever situation I am to be content. I know how to be brought low and I know how to abound. In any and every circumstance, I have learned the secret of facing plenty and hunger, abundance, and need. I can do all things through him who strengthens me." (Philippians 4: 11-13) Son, you can do all things if you persist.

Why am I writing all this? Other than sharing with you great life advice that only your mother could share, the answer is easy, because

I LOVE YOU! I love you not because it is my duty. I love you because it is what I do. You are a piece of me and I love you most times more than I love myself. My love for you is more essential than the hottest and latest toy, tech, or fashion. My love for you will outlast any person you will ever know or remember knowing. My love for you will at times seem strict and you may not like my decisions, despite those feelings I have to be your mother and perform my duties. I have always shared with you, "I am your mother first, not your friend. I do not have to be your friend, but I will always be your mother!"

I do have duties as a mother to do, prepare, restore, nurture, comfort, protect, teach; the list goes on. However, you asked me one day, 'Mommy do you like me?" I responded, "I love you!" You rebutted, "No!" "Do you like me? I know you love me?" Quickly, I replied, "YES, I like you a lot!" I may not like your reactions or your actions but I will always like you and love you, my son! My love is locked into levels unmeasurable.

I have to be realistic and consider being your mother there will be good times and bad times; as with anything. I take joy in learning you (your personality, your style, your thoughts) day in and day out and I will do my best to make the best decisions for you as you grow up and I grow older. I love you so much, I build you up, so you will not be broken easily. I teach you, so you can determine truth from lies. I show you, so you can learn from already known mistakes; this is my effort to equip you for this life. Over the years, I have been your playmate, your consoler, your confidant, your protector, your caretaker, your preparer, your cover, your giver, I am and will always be in your corner!

Tall trees have deeper roots to withstand the elements. You have been planted in love, watered with love, enduring some wind, and yet you are growing in love. Let no one stop your reach to the sky and when you touch the clouds don't stop, keep going until you mingle with the planets and stars. Push away your distraction amongst the planets and stars because there are galaxies to explore. Infinity never stops- my love is infinite-a mother's love never will stop.

With all my heart.
Love,
Mommy

God's Promise in Real Time

By Catina M. King

When thinking of writing this love letter to you my beautiful son, I couldn't help but remember the moment we found out you were coming to us. As a woman, I have always desired to have children. For a long time, I wasn't sure if that burning desire would come true due to some health issues. I accepted the fact that I may never be a mother and then my biggest dream became a reality. I was utterly shocked but then I realized that God always has a plan and he is the only one that knows when and how to make his plan come to Fruition. So, on September 26, 2015, I married your Father. Life was great and we continued trusting God with every being of our lives together. I remember September 3, 2016, I felt better than I've ever felt in my body. To this day I can't describe the feeling. September 4, 2016. I took the first of 8 Pregnancy tests…LOL before sharing with your dad. On September 9, 2016, I shared with your Dad the 8th test I took. September 12, 2016, it was confirmed that you were on the way!! That was the most exciting day of my life. It was as exciting but also scary. I was a 43-year-old becoming a "Mommy"!

My infinite love for you began the very moment I realized that you were living inside of me. We found out we were having a baby boy on October 31,2016. While we would have been happy to have a girl as well, we were extremely excited to find out we were having a boy! I always wanted a son. God really does give you your heart's desire when you delight yourself in Him. On April 27, 2017 our life as we knew it changed forever. This was your Birthdate, and this was the BEST day ever for our family. As we looked upon your face, I remembered the scripture James 1:17 "Every good and perfect gift is from above and cometh down from the Father of lights." You are our good and perfect gift son. You were created in Love, you are being raised in Love, and you will continue to grow in Love. You are a Beautiful Soul.

As a new mother it is challenging as you have this little life in your care. Knowing you are trusted with the responsibility of making sure this child is fed, bathed, changed but most importantly Loved. Needless to say, a lot of pressure for this Mommy. I wouldn't change any of the challenges as it made me stronger as your Mother. I've heard that a cord from a true Mother can't truly be separated. The love I have for you is something I cannot put into words, but I try to show you in different ways daily. You are a Strong little one and I say this with a grateful heart. Remembering scripture James 1:3 "knowing this, that the trying of your faith worketh patience." You endured a lot the first year of your life, but your strength has been so encouraging to my life as your mother. It was shortly after your birth (about 6 months) and after several appointments due to staying sick with cold-like symptoms and problems with wheezing and trying different medications that we could at your age.

One medication brought out an underlying concern that you had that was causing you to have small spasms throughout the day. No mother ever wants to see their child suffer. I was beyond terrified. My son, my baby boy was sick and there was nothing I could do. That is a mother's worst fear. No mother ever wants to feel helpless when it comes to helping their child. I was frustrated, confused, overwhelmed, emotional, and sad. After continued appointments and then a referral to a Neurology Specialist, we found out that you had what is called Infantile Spasms. That was a scary and frustrating time for our family. The unknown!! One thing that I would like you to know is that your Neurologist and his team were absolutely amazing. He was on top of beginning your treatment as quickly and as effectively as possible. You began having Treatment of injections twice a day beginning December 17, 2017. By December 24, 2017, you did not experience any more spasms. You continue to be spasm and seizure free today. This was such a trying time for us especially for you with having to have a lot of medical things completed like EEGs, an MRI's and taking preventive medications to help eliminate seizures or spasms. However, son you were super strong, and your strength continued to strengthen me. Even in your pain, you smiled through it all. You loved your time with Mommy and Daddy! As we are still going through the process of preventative measures on top of dealing with Asthma concerns you keep going like nothing is happening. You have had no delays in growth, and you continue to grow as a typical two almost-three-year-old should. It is by God's Grace that I am forever grateful and blessed.

God gave me what I needed as a Mother to get through this with you. God gave me the strength to hug your pain and face every challenge I had to face. One thing that I hope for you is to understand that Love will get you through because "God is love." You will face many challenges in life son for sure, but I know that you will go through each one gracefully because you have been taught by your parents that "God is love and He is our refuge and strength, an ever-present help in times of trouble (Psalms 46:1)."

You will have many challenges in life that will test you but, one of the biggest obstacles you will face is being a strong, Godly, African American man in this society. For sure you will deal with having to prove to others that you are the respectful young man that you will know yourself to be. You will have hurt my son, probably more than I wish you would. My prayer is that you will go through the pain, pick up the pieces and allow God to do the healing while smiling in the midst. As you grow in your gifts you will have peer pressure. Unfortunately, society has a way of making you feel irrelevant because of your skin color. Though you are not taught to judge people by their skin color, not everybody does that. Being known as a Strong, Godly, African American man is very hard in this day and time. The world presents and caters more to the bad and immoral things in life so it is always very enticing to want to be a part of it because it's what you will see. Being that Strong, Godly, African American man allows you to stand out and take precedence over all of those things. There are some who will try to mock you, some people will try to sway you by manipulation, and some people are just going to not like you at all. The blessing in all of those indiscretions is that you know who you are and what you stand for. If you always keep God first you will be an awesome Man of God, Husband, Father, Friend, and whatever you choose to be. You will have a desire to want to do what others are doing. You will even question your purpose, but my prayer is that by watching and embracing your parents' love and others that are a major part of your life you will see your purpose and the importance of taking steps to effectively grow in your purpose. Son always remember that you are Purposed for Greatness, Gifted by God, and Loved by Everyone that you encounter.

Even in all those challenges, you will need to understand the importance of keeping Christ first in your life... Very Important. Always have an open mind and the ability to show effective communication with all that you may encounter. Love with an open Heart and only allow others to love you openly with a sincere heart. My prayer is that you will always know that you can come to Mom for anything! My prayer to God is that you always know that you can communicate with me about everything! I pray that you run to my open arms always. I pray that you always know that my heart is wide open for you and that you always know that I will love you forever! My love for you is infinite. Always remember that God will always love you and never forsake you!

Mother's Love

By Lisa Millner-Little

There is a unique bond between a mother and her son. It is one of those "things that cannot be described". Even in biblical times every parent wanted a male seed. Why? Legacy! Sons carry seed to reproduce in the earth realm. This is the glory of every parent that bears a son...the name will continue to another generation. As mothers we want to raise our sons with a heightened sense of awareness of what that truly means and to break any generational curses that did not get dealt with in the father's generation. So, we love, we love them when we are correcting, chastising, frustrated with poor choices, etc. And love them just because it creates a foundation in their soul that the love we have is totally unconditional.

Once that bond is understood, our boys open up and tell us everything. Things we sometimes wish we never knew but so glad they have entrusted us with their heart, time and space to be vulnerable. We are a safe place. Nonjudgmental but truthful, sometimes brutally honest. Our sons realize that I may not like what she has to say but I know she would not steer me wrong.

A mother's love is instructional. We are the GPS for their life until they can ultimately find their way. Our sons even when unspoken questions want to know how we feel about things, what is our insight, foresight, and/or experiences with the subject matter at hand. We have to be intentional on what and how we release our story. Be honest, sincere, and encourage your son that life is about challenges, but he is more than able to conquer any mountain that stands before him. We can be too strict at times but we know the world is waiting to literally in doctrine them with teaching we abhor! So we want them to read, understand, comprehend so we create flashcards, we sit and google math problems for formulas, etc. because we want their best self to be seen by others. My boys are from one extreme to the other. My oldest is diligent, hardworking, and what he gets he earned it because he worked for it. My youngest son is flamboyant, the life of the party, let me do what is needed and move on to my social life. With these dynamics under one roof...whew...you must have a system that works. Well, mine was trial and error. I had to be fair, across the board with my requirements and without comparison. I never wanted my children to feel as if they needed to compete with each other but to love and appreciate their individualities. So, we implement an instructional guide for minimum requirements which evolved as they matured in age. The rules were across the board point blank. I needed them to understand that any decision comes with a consequence whether good or bad. Rules are rules and the world is full of them!

A mother's love is instinctive. We can sense that something is not quite right even when they are not around us. I remember when my oldest son had left for college, I was so bothered that he was not emotional about leaving me as I was him. I had to go down the following week to drop off some supplies and I mentioned that "I was in my feelings" regarding his actions. He kindly informed me that I should not have been because I raised him with that day in mind and if he needed me, he knew I would be present! I had to cut my apron strings on that very day and begin to really trust God with what he had entrusted to me. I found out that my mother's instinct was heightened when I stepped back, not peeping over his shoulder, nagging him etc. My prayer then became Lord, teach me how to release him into this world but keep me sensitive to your voice regarding his progress as a man. To my surprise, the day came, and I kept seeing him in a dream (I'm not a dreamer by the way) and he was always looking indecisive. After about three days of this, I called him and began to talk and reiterate his purpose and his assignment. Affirming that I believed in him and how proud I was of the man he was becoming with being responsible and making wise decisions. Of course, the initial response was yes ma'am, I know, thank you ma…But in the same week he called wanted to know if we could talk, he began to pour out his heart and thank me for being present! Always on point and not just brushing my gut instincts off. As much as they aspire to be independent we still know that we are needed now more than ever to be a sounding board and an advisor on how to proceed to their next level. Mother's even if it is late in the midnight hour follow your instinct your sons' life could very well be dependent on your obedience to follow up.

A mother's love is intentional. Intentionality increases influence, and influence is something God asks us to be intentional about. We cannot underestimate the power of mother love, the value of home, and the significance of our intentional presence in the lives of our sons. The profession of motherhood is all about influence. You and I have an incredible opportunity to influence the next generation by what we do as a mother every day. Good parents aren't perfect. There's no formula to follow, but there are ways you can grow every day. Are there days I have failed as a parent yes; I've made mistakes but even in those times I have been intentional about asking for forgiveness with my sons and getting back on track with evolving as a parent and growing from my mistakes. I'm intentional about keeping open conversations going even if it is a decision that I must make for the well-being of my family but uncomfortable for my sons. Being intentional means, you have foresight. You are reviewing, analyzing every possible situation, and choosing the plan with the least impact on your seed. Honestly, there are times when "it is what it is" let's then make this a teachable moment because one day our sons will be head of households and there are more no's than yes's in life but you have to learn how to maneuver on the road less traveled to come out if nothing into something beautiful! This builds your son's character and integrity.

We are the voice of influence in our son's life! We are shaping them more with our actions and not our words. They watch us, they are in tune with us so we must remain intentional with explanations of circumstances, questions that make us blush, and with our influence direct them to the correct paths of life.

A mother's love is inspiring. We are our sons' first role models. We display daily sacrifice, strength, stamina, and patience. I love the song by Chaka Khan..." I'm every woman it's all in me". We are demonstrating in everyday life that we possess these qualities and they are in a full demonstration. We are the first women they love, and it is imperative that we are inspiring our sons to be themselves. I'm passionate and excited when I see their development and I acknowledge it to both in different ways. We celebrate wins and discuss losses to get the lessons. Eventually, our sons will be leaders in various capacities: home, community, business, church to name a few. So we must inspire them to be their best self in all situations because as a visionary they must be able to communicate and be principled in their agenda. Inspiration is a strong influencer of encouragement to build our sons self-esteem and allow them to seek out their purpose.

A mother's love is innovative. We are thinkers! Sometimes we overthink situations and it can be frustrating. My sons tell me sometimes Ma, pump your breaks. But the truth of the matter is we are showing them how to look at all aspects before deciding. And sometimes to get the outcome you desire you must think outside of the box. Just because XYZ did it that way doesn't mean you have to! We prod their minds with questions, revelations, ideas and we watch the development/growth of their mindset begin to stretch, sometimes change and expand in ways that are mind blowing. Being innovative we assist them in seeking roads less traveled which develops their leadership skills, problem solving capabilities, and becoming strategic with the "what if's" that will occur.

You must remember you have sons not machines we can't just give out only "to-do list" they are not machines. Realizing with innovation that we are intentional in building our sons because we know that, eventually machines break! We nurture their personal growth, perspective, and perceptions with creativity, passion, and enthusiasm. We make sure that our sons have balance. They become well rounded and inquisitive for the better. Better lives, careers, desires and to always want better for themselves. We love them into a place of personal innovation and the funny thing is they don't even realize it. These are seeds of righteousness that shall yield forth a harvest that will leave a legacy in their children's children.

I believe God knew exactly what he was doing when he created a woman and then opened her womb to carry and birth a son. God himself in the beginning of time established the hierarchy of the home God being the head and Man (our sons) over the family. Proverbs 1:8-9 states 8 Listen, my son, to your father's instruction and do not forsake your mother's teaching. 9 They are a garland to grace your head and a chain to adorn your neck. God has he equipped us to be teachers through love to make sure their heads (minds) are secure and to protect their hearts. We understand that our love has the ability to be the voice of God in our sons' life. A voice of reason but one of determination. With the intent that limitless is really a word! They can keep creating, building, evolving into ALL that God put in their heart.

I have never neglected not to daily affirm my sons in and out of their presence with these words to the Lord: May Jeron and Justin be ten times greater than the men in the world in wisdom, knowledge, character and understanding and integrity. May they be men of standard and valor in the face of adversity. May they uphold a standard of living where men will inquire of their God!

Our love has the power to change nations one son at a time. I believe in the power of love because it was love that redeemed us from the curse of the law and has given us the victory through Jesus Christ. Our love is so potent that we can mother sons we did not birth and have the same effect upon their lives as well. We are "built for this" before the foundations of the world.

I love what our creator has allowed us to create, nurture, uplift, build, impart, correct, empower, and stabilize so our sons can go from boys to men!

I love you forever until my breath leaves my body…

Jeron and Justin Keen!

Love,
Moma

Mother's Love

By Juandalynn Jones-Hunt

Dear son,

I don't know how to fully express my love for you, about you, or because of you. What I do know is that my whole world changed when you became a part of it, and it continues to revolve around you. My perspectives were altered, and my passion was displaced. What must have seemed important prior to you is difficult to remember. I can hardly recall my life or its purpose before you. When people ask me to describe who I am, it is impossible to do so without referencing myself as your mother. To put it simply, son, you are my everything.

One might think that to be totally consumed with the love and care of another is too dear of a cost to pay, because it robs one of their entire existence. Even understanding that fact, I was and am still willing to accept the task and privilege of being your mother through the good times and the bad times; the happy and the sad; in sickness and in health; through life and beyond death; and financial struggle or wealth.

Wealth is something I know little about, as I have spent your lifetime pouring all my love, time, and funds into you and your well-being and happiness. Frankly, I would pour even more into you if I had it to give. I know that I do too much for you, while my love for you makes it difficult for me to dial it back. Forgive me, son.

Forgive me for trying to protect you from the uncertainties, the evils, and the disappointments of life. I am guilty of loving you too dearly and for holding you too tightly, because I love you so deeply and fully. I understand that I should have stepped back more often to allow you to make your own mistakes, to stumble, to fail and to grow more independently. I believe in you and I know that you are equipped with all that you need to succeed. I just fear that I find my sole purpose in serving you. As I mentioned earlier, my sole purpose is to love you. Forgive me for learning how to parent while I tarried along the way savoring every moment. I didn't always know what to do or how to do, but we got through. Me and you. Do not be mistaken, your father's role was a mighty one regarding the shaping of you, but heaven called him away sooner than we could imagine. Alas, it is just us two. If I had it all to do over again, I would gladly travel this same path with you, my dear. My reason for waking and for being is because of you and my motivation and inspiration for being is my love for you.

This is a mother's love. To see you aspire to have more than I have, to achieve more than I have, to be happier more than I have known, to be fully protected in all that you do, to live in calm and not chaos, and to love more than I loved; is all that I pray for each night and it is the substance of all that I whisper throughout the day.

This is a mother's love.

With all my love,
Mom

Race

Since I am black should I be proud?

Should I be scared because I am an African American male that tries to succeed in life?

Should I be scared that I may not make it home every night?

This is my race.

The world thinks it is funny to put me in my place but it is not.

That is not how I was taught.

Because of the things you brought

and the things that are put in my mind that make me blind.

You may say "Oh it is easy to be black." but it is not.

The only one that know are me, myself, and I so please don't tell that lie.

This is my race.

The world thinks it is funny to put me in my place but it is not.

Ocir Black

Being a Black Man in America

By Sondra Trice-Jones

I remember wanting a boy when I found out I was with a child. I thought- it will be much easier with a boy, no hair to comb, no ribbons to match with outfits, no competitiveness amongst girls. Boys love their mothers I thought. He will grow up and be my forever protector.

My son was born in January 1994. It was freezing that winter and I was in a very dark place! He was gorgeous, born with chocolate skin and deep blue eyes, I later found out that all the men are born with deep blue eyes that turn to brown and when they become seniors they turn back to the deep blue hue! I was so grateful he was healthy and was ready to get him home and settled in. Now that I'm older and wiser, I realize we were essentially homeless as I did not have my name on a lease anywhere and home was at my parents' house. They welcomed us with open arms and showered him with more than he needed as they helped me get on my feet.

Oh, I named him Jonathan Geordan Lee Thomas. I did not want him to have his father's middle name George, and definitely wanted him to be named after my father so I included Lee! He was the best baby ever! So sweet and well behaved! You only had to tell him something once and he got it especially about danger and strangers. Over the years, all I ever received about him was positive feedback! I stayed on him to be the very best and he always came back with just enough. I learned to stop complaining and work on acceptance as he was still exhaling into the world more than I had ever given at this point. See I had a drug problem that spiraled out of control from 1985-1997, with the help of my little one; I got clean and have stayed clean for 23 years now. By then he was 3yrs old. When I came out of that fog I promised myself that I would be all I could be to my family and started to create a new way of life. With the help of my father, I taught my boy chivalry, how to stand up for himself with his words and to always, always be respectful to girls/women and never get physical with a girl no matter what. Things started really looking up for us around 2001. We divorced his father and moved to an area that I had to work hard to afford but was determined to be in for the sake of my son. I wanted him to have the best and to experience a lifestyle that I felt we both deserved. I put him in private school and when I was short with tuition I would work at the front office to make up the difference. I ended up opening up my own business and even though time management was a struggle for me I made sure to keep Jon extra busy. I recently found out that my son wanted to be called Jon because he actually did not like being named after his father. My favorite saying is "some things take forever to discover." My boy learned to navigate through the majority white private school making friends and becoming pretty popular playing basketball. I remember when he first started having issues with his vision and was concerned about wearing glasses to school. He told me, "I'm the shortest of all my friends and now I can't see." I responded, "if they tease you, tell them I can see better than you, I've got four eyes and you only got two." He came home that day and when asked how school was he said "it was fine, nobody bothered me." "Thank God I didn't have to use that saying you told me!" At this point, he was graduating from junior high school and except for some subtle statements like does everyone in your family do the electric slide line dance and a few issues when he dated white girls he was doing great. He went on to public high school and there he was subjected to marijuana and dressing to fit in. I expressed my dislike for any of that I told him if I ever hear about you walking around with your pants down past your waste and smoking weed I would be up at that school with no bra on, rollers in my hair and my slippers on escorting him around all day and introducing myself to his peers as his mother. You want to act ghetto well so can I. If he indulged he made sure to keep it from me. His first speeding ticket was a 17 and I used the scared straight tactic and had him thinking he was going to jail if he didn't find a way to earn the money to pay for it by the time his court date came around and he was still one hundred and fifteen dollars short. By the time my son started College he had escaped most things that his peers had got caught up into. To this day he has never had a fight, never sold drugs and never been to jail. He's shared his stories regarding racism and discrimination. Nothing is worth your life and don't you ever forget that I say. Ignorance is worth ignoring and if you can't, call your mother I will handle it. He smiles….I'm a grown man mom. The thing that upsets him the most is police violence against black men. He is not sure how to navigate around it and I don't know if I have an answer for him either. He's expressed, there is nothing you can really do to stay alive if confronted, you could die if you put your hands up, you could die if you don't roll your window down, you could die if you reach for your registration, you could die if you use your phone to record, you could die if you get out the car, you could die if you stay in the car…I just want to be able to make it back home to my wife and daughter and that phone call I expect from you every night…

Being a Black Man in America

From a Mother's Perspective

By Tomeka A. Wormack

To my amazing young king,

What do I want you to know about being a black male. Being born black and a male seems as if you have automatic strikes against you. The negative connotation about Black men was already set before you were born. So, before you even took your first breath into this world, we were already setting the stage to help you overcome these obstacles that would be placed on you by society. What do I know about being a Black Male in America? Technically, I don't know because I am a woman. However, I know what I hear and what I see. I also know from a woman's perspective what I would want in and from a Black man in America.

Over time, generations change, maturity level changes, and even expectations which require a different set of standards for each level change. My dad has been blessed to see 81 years of life. He still lives in Wilmington and I make a point to talk to him several times a week. I've heard him tell me stories about different encounters as a black male, both being young and old. I decided to ask him during one of our many conversations, " Dad, tell me what it was like growing up as a black man in America and what would you say about it now in this day and age".

In his early 20s, he had to endure segregation. Despite those circumstances, he attended college, Fayetteville State University, and graduated with a degree in teaching. He started his teaching career at an integrated school and at one point was the only Black male teacher. Thankfully, he was a black male that did not succumb to his circumstances or stereotype. It wasn't uncommon to see them shining shoes on the side.

He did express the indifference of treatment and stereotypes placed on the black male then and now. However, he does feel that there are more job opportunities for you to take advantage of with higher paying positions. You no longer have to only be the trash man, butler, carpenter, brick layer, or whatever you feel was only good to work as a black male. Now you can be whatever you want to be if you put your mind to it.

Did you know, son, that black men are more likely than your non-black counterparts to be pulled over, searched and arrested? There have been so many incidences of young kings in the news, taken away from their families too soon, whether by death or imprisonment. Now some things are by our own fault but you have the tools you need to overcome those odds.

One thing we prepare you for at birth, literally, is making sure you get a good education and having high intelligence before you start.

Although we do the best we can, it still does not negate the fact that, no matter how educated you are, you are more likely to be disciplined in school. That is why we always try to encourage you to pay attention, listen in school, so it gives no reason for them to raise an eyebrow your way.

"Make sure you go to college and get you a good education so you can get a good job". That is the old familiar cliché' that will never get old. Unfortunately, son, the reality is that you can have one of the best jobs in the highest paid corporations/organization, but more likely to lose your job or make less than your non-black counterparts. It is not fair but it is reality.

Have you ever heard of the phrase, " one bad apple spoils the bunch"? Because of the " bad apples ", black men have been judged, or painted a picture of being intimidating, violent in nature, "scary". Some may think if they are wearing locs, sagging pants, or even heavy jewelry are less intelligent. However, this is not a true indicator of that but presentation and first impression means everything.

I had come across a post on Instagram one day. It was about a young black male that attended East Illinois University, not to mention he was on the swim team. He seemed to appear to be a very distinguished young educated man. The team had stopped at a rest stop for a bathroom break. He was walking back to the team bus when 6 officers pulled up on him. They threw him to the ground, put a knee on his neck, guns drawn to his head and life threatened. Why? They claimed they thought he was a suspect that had fled or was holding the bus hostage. This is a young African American athlete that attends a prestigious university only to be mistreated by law enforcement.

What does being a Black male in America mean? Let's reflect on a few things that seem to be our reality. Being a black male means not being able to freely jog in a white neighborhood without being chased by two white men with weapons thinking and assuming you were the one who " did it ". Being a black male means not being able to walk to the store a night time with a black hoodie on to grab a bottle of tea and a pack of Skittles, only to be murdered on your way back home by a coward who wanted to play law enforcer because he's intimidated and looked " suspicious".. Being a Black male means not being able to have anything externally malfunctioning on your luxury car without being stopped and harassed, although on your way to the auto part store to get what you need to get it fixed. It means not being able to shop around in the store with a BB gun for purchase and phone in the other hand without being falsely accused of waving it in the air, pointing it at others or displaying some sort of threatening behavior. Thank God for the security cameras and witnesses to dispute the accusations.

Being a Black Male in America means not being able to walk out of Walmart before being questioned, another mistaken identity case. Being a black male means not being able to stand by your disabled car as you wait for help to arrive without something detrimental happening. Being Black means not being able to drive in the suburbs with your family in the care, then being pulled over by police, asked for license and registration, being honest enough to the officer know you have a licensed weapon in the car, only to be mistaken as reaching for it, then being shot and killed right in front of your family, who is also in the car. Being a black male means not being able to sit in your own apartment, minding your own business, eating ice cream, without being mistaken as an intruder IN YOUR OWN HOME by a supposedly fatigued female police officer who thought she was going into her apartment. Last but not least, being a Black Male in America means not being able to live at home, with your mom in a good neighborhood, playing your video game 10 o'clock at night, hearing a loud bang at the front door only find an off duty officer in uniform with a gang of non- law enforcement Caucasian people behind him with assault weapons on the other side of the door. They try to force their way into the home but eventually find out that they are at the wrong home. Makes you wonder what was going to happen if they were at the right person's house. We already know or can conclude what would've happened. It should never be acceptable for any young or older Black male in America to feel unsafe and disrespected anywhere in this world and unfortunately too many live through it. What can I say? It's never going to be easy.

I know you may not want to hear about those situations. I don't tell you these things to make you afraid to live but I do want you to be aware of what is going on in the world. Be mindful of how you carry yourself. You must stay vigilant of your surroundings and even the people you deal with. I'm sure you are thinking, well, is there anything positive about being a Black Male in America? Of course it is. You are a Black King and your Black Queen awaits so that you may build a strong tribe together. What advice do I give? As I've always strongly encouraged, strive to get your education and apply yourself. Be a go-getter because no one will hand it to you. If anything, you actually have to work a little bit harder at achieving your goal. Learn more about your community, how and what you can do to help make it a better place. Always try to do the right thing and treat fellow man right. I continue to encourage you to save money as you earn it and give God his portion. Last but never least, as always, read your Word and develop a strong relationship with God. Continue to pray and ask God for His protection, guidance, and discernment in every situation and at all times. As a mother, my prayers and undying love for you will never cease. Remember son, you're not just a Black Male in America, you are a Black King in America. So adjust your crown and hold your head high.

" Don't let anyone look down on you because you are young, but set an example for the believers in speech, in conduct, in love, in faith and in purity." - 1 Timothy 4:12

" Be on your guard; stand firm in the faith; be courageous; be strong" - 1 Corinthians 16:13

Love,

Mom

Being a Black Man in America

By Juandalynn Jones-Hunt

Dear son,

I wanted to reflect upon being a Black man in America. So often we are reminded of the struggle of what it is like to be a Black man in the nation of opportunity, the nation of promise, and the nation of plenty. The Black man is othered and too often categorized and classified as oppressed and defeated. I dare you, my son, to broaden your eyes and your mind to seeing the Black man in America, differently.

Being a Black man in America requires grit. The kind of grit that surpasses misconceptions, misinformed judgements, and miseducation. Being a Black man in America requires one to be doubly qualified, where being capable isn't enough. Being a capable Black man gets you in the room, but having grit to transform one into the position of being a "standout", is what gets you through the door. Because you are Black, you must prove more, do more, be more, work more, advocate more, and remind folk more often that you were capable when you started. Being capable isn't enough while being Black.

Being a Black man in America requires patience. Patience is necessary when navigating these waters. In American, a Black man has to maintain patience for understanding why others see him as a threat when he has yet to approach them, has to maintain patience for understanding why he is the victim of hate when he comes in love, has to maintain patience for understanding why he is first described by his outer appearance instead of his inner heart, or has to maintain patience for understanding how his mind is free in a world that wants to keep him captive with limitations and restrictions set only for the containment and impedance of the Black man in America.

Being a Black man in American means that you ought to be reminded of your history and heritage. You must remember that you are the derivative of African kings and queens while also being a descendant of American slaves. You must remember to be prideful and humble at the same time. You must remember that you are left to tarry the road they trotted and to carry the torch that lights the road to guide your own footsteps and to serve as a beacon for those who follow you. Son, hold your light and hold it high for your brother my need you, as he is lost in the storm. You must remember to be your brothers' keeper along the way. This world may label you and categorize you as they will, but understand and claim your greatness for you are full of grit, patience, and a legacy that declares you to be who is more than capable of all he seeks to accomplish for himself and his community. Therefore, it is an honor and a privilege to be a Black man in America.

With all my pride,

Mom

Change the World

My dear sons,
The world sees threat
The world sees fear
The world sees a life that is not dear

Your world is love
Your world is kind
Your world is hope
Built with God's design

Your steps will create
Your steps will shape
Your steps will force
The world to see

Men with Character
Men with Heart
Men with Purpose
Men of Color

D. JaMese M. Black

Your Future Matters:
And, it Begins Now!

By Shanta Y. Jackson

Dear Sons,

I look at you and see me! From your cheek bones to that appeasing personality to your quick wit and drive but also, the procrastination, the second guessing of yourself, that "not trying something because you might not be great at it" thing. Yep, that is me too.

I did not see myself in you right away. But as you both developed and grew, there I was staring back at my hopes, dreams, and fears.

And, as I look, I know that I do not want you to take my same road in life. You two mean too much to me for me to stand still and do nothing. Your future is important, and it starts now.

My story is one that I am proud of. After a career-changing diagnosis of nodules on my vocal cords which led me to quit the teaching profession, I was left reeling. What would I do now? How will I make money? All I had ever dreamed of centered around academia and I didn't know what to do.

I was left feeling like my purpose was no longer relevant. I floated through life for a few years until real estate found me. The knowledge that I would be helping and educating people moved me in a real way. But, the inner journey to get there was difficult simply because it asked more of me than I had to give.

You must have confidence, a true sense of self and a faith so strong that it dulls all your fears and I just was not in full supply of any of these items.

I had always felt that I was a good person, but I never thought I was a "deserving" person. And, let me tell you, for your future to be bright, you must first believe that you are WORTHY to have a great future. That is what they don't tell you. You must believe it is possible *before* it is possible.

After starting my career and feeling like I was risking it all, I made mistake after mistake and finally found my way. But this does not mean I am done.

As I see it, after being in real estate for 15 years, my stagnation is embarrassing to me. If I am being honest, it's embarrassing because I was in and I was out for several years. I was constantly questioning myself. I was never fully invested because I was scared to succeed. I know it seems strange, but I was quite alright with failure and the status quo. I could talk myself out of feeling bad, I was used to failure. Failure felt comfortable because it would always be there. Success was unattainable in my eyes. My dream for you is that you recognize your greatness early, to trust God and yourself and to live passionately because your future matters to me and this world.

I do not want you wasting precious time like I did. Where would I be now if I had the self-confidence, the faith, and the self-awareness.

So, sons, start now!!

When It feels like I am on you for no reason, there is a true reason behind it. I want you to have the confidence to know that you can do anything you put your mind to in life. Confidence comes from winning. I want you to get used to winning. Not so you can feel superior but so you can understand that you CAN win.

I know you hate it when I turn all our conversations into conversations about grades and goals but there is a reason behind it. School is one of the first places you gain confidence. Student achievement is about believing you can be great and then putting in the work. Rinse and repeat. And, when this happens again you create a pattern of success. Grades are important, yes! But, the experiences in obtaining those grades gives you more. School is just an exercise or precursor to life. I procrastinated writing papers in school, and I procrastinated in making life decisions as well. One thing can directly lead to another. So, begin now to do all you can to build your confidence so that when you are faced with challenges, you can pull from other times when you conquered it all.

Do and be. I see you wanting to do certain activities but fearful of not being good at it or being the best. I need you to stretch yourself. Only in the stretching will you learn more about yourself. Tackle that next thing and put your all into it whether you believe you will excel in it. Being in a comfortable position can lead to a dead zone. In a dead zone there is no growth, there is a complacency that takes over your spirit and quashes all your dreams. In the dead zone, you don't wonder about things, you don't invest and seek out new challenges because it is easier and safer to do what you always have done. Sons, I know you see your greatness, but you can't exercise it until you have put it to work. Do what it takes and be aware of its effects on you.

Gaining self- awareness and confidence will pull you further into accomplishing whatever you want to accomplish. However, add growing your faith to the list as well. Fear has been a factor in almost every decision in my life. Fear was so close to me it felt like a family member. It caused me to turn down some great opportunities, fear held me back from speaking my truth and fear constantly whispered in my ear self-doubting messages. I was and am still battling that internal battle with myself. I want you so aware of God's goodness that fear is a non-factor in your future. I want you to go after whatever you want to do with vigor and passion and believe that you can be great.

Sons, your futures are bright! I can see that from a million miles away. And, I am going to do everything in my power to instill this message. I am on a mission to break all generational curses of mediocre achievement, self-doubt, and fear. Your future matters to your family and to the world and now is the time to begin!!

Your Future Matters

If I Knew Then What I Know Now

By Tomeka A. Wormack

Growing up, the one thing we hesitate on is listening to our parents. As I often try to give good sound advice, it's the constant battle of feeling as if you don't know what you're talking about. If I've said it once, I've said it a million times. " Son, you do know I didn't come out of the womb at the age I am now right?". We've already gone through what you may possibly encounter as you travel your journey called life. We live and learn and those mistakes we've made, we dare not have you go through the same thing if we can help it.

Since you were a child and able to understand, I've always tried to encourage you to be self-sufficient while at the same time very nurturing. I want you to understand that everything you do, every decision you make, will ultimately affect your future. "Make wise decisions" and "if I had only known then what I know now" are often quotes that are drilled into your head.

As we embark on a new stage of life and journey to High School, I reflect on the advice given to me around that same age. I also was highly intelligent and had to think about what I wanted to do in the future. My dad was a teacher and my mom worked in a manufacturing plant. I don't think I realized the importance of my decisions then that would be an astounding change in my life now. An example I now find myself giving to my son is one of choosing to enhance my college career or staying with friends during the summer because we would be parting ways after graduation. I received an invitation to participate in the Honors Summer Program at Winston Salem State University after I was accepted. The starting date was June 13, 1997 and I was graduating on June 12, 1997. Hard decision to make considering I wouldn't be able to spend any time at all with my friends and we were all going to different schools. My parents explained to me how great of any honor that would be and reflects well on a resume'. I am forever grateful that I listened to them. I took an English and Math class during that summer prior to starting my actual Freshman year which counted towards my college credits. I was invited again the next summer which allowed me to be ahead of the game. I was able to complete school and obtain my nursing degree in 4 years. With that said, choosing the high school and college to go should not be a decision based on where all your friends are going or who has the coolest colors but which will provide the best opportunities to help you be successful in life.

The next phase of life is going to college. Not everybody is college material and that is okay. However, you must do something positive with your life and hopefully have a great impact on many people around you or even the world. For those that do want to attend college, there is usually a favorite college they want to attend. I tend to offer the advice of choosing your college based off of what you want your degree in. Then research the college with the best program. Never choose a college without thinking about if a good program exists to support you to be a successful student and then graduate.

When asking a young boy what he would like to grow up to be, many times I would hear, " I want to be a professional football player" or some sort of professional athlete. I would cringe on the inside every time that I would hear that statement. I would often stress the importance of getting a good education or a degree for backup. I'd say to them, " well what if you hurt your knee, then what would you have to fall back on?" They usually shrug their shoulders because they haven't thought that far. I'm sure they have the assumption that things will work out for sure. I will always encourage you to think about what you may want to do in life because essentially that will be your career likely for the rest of your working life. Make sure it will be something you enjoy and that when you leave your workplace, you can sleep at night with a peace of mind.

With that said, it is so important to weigh your options and think about what may come out of the decisions you make now that can and will affect your future. I don't want you to be so precise in thinking about every single thing that you forget to have a life but detailed enough to know what's important. You know we often have discussions about life in general even down to choosing a mate. As parents, our job is to raise and protect you, to send you out into this crazy world to be an upstanding citizen in America supplied with most of the tools needed to take on life. I don't have all the answers but I can guide you to the resources.

I hope that you will gain much insight on how you should conduct your mind, your thoughts and actions. As you grow, you will face many challenges that I know you can overcome. Remember to always keep God first and look to the hills which your help comes from as the old folks say. If you find yourself in a bind, never hesitate to ask for help or guidance because again, one wrong decision could turn your whole life around. It may be a change that can never be repaired.

A challenge you may face are the people who you choose to be in your circle. " Choose your friends wisely" or "birds of a feather flock together" my mother and many others close to me would say. I often find myself repeating that many times with hopes that you too will listen. It's called a "friend check" . The people in your circle will become your second family and the ones that you hope will be there along your journey to the future. You definitely want them to be genuine, Godly minded, have your back and best interest at heart, and just good respectful people in general. This also goes for the spouse that you will choose to spend the rest of your life with.

It's important to take care of yourself mentally, spiritually, financially and physically. Countless times, I encourage going to the Bible or pray when things are bothering you. When your mind is cluttered with the daily boggles of life, it's hard to think clearly or make sound judgement that can affect future decisions and outcomes. Save money and don't forget to give God his portion for we truly know who truly holds our future. Eat right and exercise. Get regular check ups at the doctor. What you put in your body will either feed the disease or fight the disease and early detection is the key to treatment. How can you enjoy your future if you don't take care of yourself. The choice to breastfeed was one of the greatest gifts I could ever give with hopes to jumpstart a healthy future. Continuing to encourage you to make healthy lifestyle decisions and staying active is something I'll never stop doing because I always want you to live a long life.

Be knowledgeable about many topics, especially politics. Know who is running for the different positions and what their values are. It will be up to you to help hold this nation accountable because, again, they will affect your future. Be aware of the laws and vote for what is right and just. Get involved in the community because one day the community will be taking care of you in one way or another.

As a child, I always followed my dad everywhere he went and watched everything he did. He was always doing an odd job for someone whether it be a family member, friend, neighbor, church member or whoever. Once I was living on my own, anything that was broken or needed to be put together, I remembered the skills I had picked up from him. I try to instill those same values to this day. I figure when you are out on your own, you too will know how to fix a broken toilet handle, put together a cabinet, or perhaps, something as simple as planting a garden. If you don't know how to do it, you always have YouTube and go from there. Helping my dad and learning how to do odd jobs is something that I will forever cherish and be grateful for. It allowed me to pass these skills on so that they can be used in the future. I encourage frequent calls and communications with the patriarchs of your family or any positive role models, hang around them and observe. Sometimes great life lessons are learned and good advice that I hope travels with you in life always.

My intention of this information is for you to use it and make your future matter. I hope that you learn from this and will pass this along to your children and others for many generations to come. Be a key piece in society not just another citizen. Anything you put your mind to, I know it will be accomplished and change the world for the better. Remember your future matters but never let your past determine what that holds for you.

"Your Mental Health is the Heartbeat of Your Life"

By Catina M. King

"Loving who you are"

It took me some time to get an understanding of this title. It is crucial that every human being understands what mental health is and how it can affect one's life. The intricate details of someone's mental health and how it can affect someone's life is by far one of the most important aspects in life. What is Mental Health?? The exact definition of "mental health" is the level of a person's psychological wellbeing or an absence of mental illness. To the point that you are able to function at a satisfactory level of emotions and behavioral adjustment My thought of your mental health being the heartbeat of your life is you are responsible for protecting it. What are you protecting? You must have a strong belief in who you are and what you stand for. You must be grounded in knowing who you are. So, son, laugh out loud! I've always heard that laughter is good for the soul and the best medication for stress. That statement brings me great joy because your laughter son is so addictive. Your laugh is so refreshing, and you laugh so freely! I know that you may not understand your laughter now, but I believe in my spirit that God is using you even at your young age to brighten the days of others.

When you meet others there is joy. I am not saying this because you are my son (even though it is a bonus..lol). I am saying this because your spirit is so captivating. You are so much like your father. We call you our social butterfly and mood changer. Even in our challenging days and not so happy moments, you have the ability to turn that around. Laughter always seems to bring greater happiness, it has been known to lighten burdens, it has brought about hope to those in great despair. Son, your laughter has allowed you to have an awesome connection with other people. Your laughter seems to keep you grounded. So, keep laughing, and enjoy it when you do because as I stated earlier your laughter is infectious. One day your laughter will heal someone's wounded soul.

There are things and cares in this world that will drive you crazy or at least make you feel like it. You will learn for sure that there are different journeys that you will face in life, the good and the bad. If you keep Christ in your life through your journey you will have no choice but to make it through. Always strive to be the best by doing your best. Understanding that you are not expected to be perfect and that you cannot do things on your own. Just know that you can ask for help and learn to receive that help with a Grateful Heart. Avoid negative social life and do not allow negativity to consume your life. Be careful of the energy you allow around you. People are sponges and if they are exhibiting negative energy you can be a sponge that absorbs that energy. Remember this my beautiful son, if you surround yourself around negativity and allow your thoughts to be rooted in that negativity then a tree of aggravation and frustration with spring forth. This will add unnecessary stress and confusion. Remember that we need others in our lives to help keep us grounded and in some ways accountable. Also, remember that we need to keep honest and cheerful "company" that can add to us not take from us. Sometimes in life, we cannot choose our circumstances, but we can choose what we allow in our lives. Always remember the scripture that you should "cast your care on God because he loves you and cares for you (1 Peter 5:7)."

My final wish for you, son, is that you always embrace your education, keep learning and empower yourself with education and wisdom and I assure you, your future will be bright. When I was younger my home life was stressful, and it lacked confidence. I didn't realize how much until later in life. I learned that my home wasn't protected as it should have been or could have been. My parents did their best for what they knew. I knew that education was important but lacked structure and it hurt me in many ways. Along the way, I realized the importance of education and began to seek the knowledge and wisdom that I needed to have a successful life. So, I made a brave decision to go back to school and it has been my second-best decision I ever made. Of course, my son was my first best decision. I want you to be different. I do not want you to waste your best years not valuing education. A child discovering a world of education is a beautiful gesture. Something I want you to experience. I never want you to have to play catch-up or feel that you didn't seize the opportunities bestowed upon you as a child. In your education know that there is help and never be afraid to ask for it. Remember asking for help does not make you beneath anyone else, it just states that you believe in yourself and have enough nerve to know what you need. Always take care of yourself and your mental health. Go as far as your heart desires but do not make unrealistic goals that will cause you to give up. Trust the process which includes trusting God. Find peace, purpose, and strength in your educational decisions with the help of your loving parents, close friends, school supports, but most of all with God. Do this in prayer daily as God will see you through it all. This will prepare you for great leadership. Remembering this scripture, "write the vision and make it plain" (Habakkuk 2:2) Always have vision son. Never do anything that you do not want to be done to you. Being a leader is not so much about what you do but about who you are and how you act. As I have stated throughout this writing. You must always seek guidance from God in how you can grow in your life and any leadership role you are in. Remember that when you advise, encourage or, give any part of yourself, you are displaying Leadership. May your leadership impact others in a positive manner. It's going to be vital for you, son to keep your mental awareness centered on what you believe. Living in this world there are things that will try to consume you especially with what society or the things going on at the time will offer. There will be so many ill vices out there that will try to dictate, distract, or control you. My beautiful son, you have been chosen to be a leader and an example to all those you meet young and old. You have touched many lives in the short time you have been here, and you bring joy to all that encounter your personality. You have a smile that lights up a room. Always remember that your mental health and its stability will allow you to stay centered as you form the life you chose to live and the life that revolves around you. Never forget that keeping God first in your life will allow you to deal with the situations and the trials that are going to come up against you!

Life is going to bring to you many achievements, many pleasures, many relationships, many trials, many disappointments along with many opportunities. My sweet boy, do not allow all of your successes, disappointments, or setbacks to consume your mind. If you allow these things to consume you, then you will allow them to enslave you mentally and you will become one dimensional. So, I leave you with a quote that your father shared with me given to him by your grandfather "Chester King " he stated that he would always say "Let nothing consume your mind. Be it money, sex, drugs, women, love, successes or, failures." Always trust yourself, live for yourself but most of all, always love yourself.

My Dearest Son-

A reflection letter to my teenage son

By Ruthmarie B. Mitchell

Your ability to cope with the ups and downs that life will always present are key factors in your ability to navigate through life. Over time I will teach you how to meditate and pray in a quiet place to check your own pulse. Only you will know best the adjustments to make in order to meet the demands that life will throw your way. Always be in tune with your thoughts and feelings.

As a Black male you are taught that by nature you are angry. I need you to understand that because you are human you have every single emotion inside of you and you owe it to yourself to express how you feel, but in a way that is healthy for your wellbeing and overall success. It is okay to cry, be angry, feel sad, be mad. It is not okay to bottle up your feelings, hide from them, or fear that you are weak in expressing any of these perceived negative emotions. It is okay and important for you to reach out for help when you start to become overwhelmed with the obstacles that often come from living. It is okay and wise to seek counseling, get the help you need, and even take medication while working on negative thoughts and behaviors through therapy. This is by far not a sign of weakness, but rather a sign of greatness.

Every season of your life will present new challenges and sometimes an overwhelming emotional state. The way that you choose to handle the emotions that come along for the ride will determine the outcome. Your state of mind is more than half the battle in any situation that life brings, expected or not. Remember that it is just a moment in time, even when it seems like an eternity. It is an opportunity for growth and a time to gain wisdom before the next set of challenges present themselves. With each new season, remind yourself of how you successfully made it through the last challenge that also at that moment, seemed impossible. Give yourself permission to feel all of the emotions that come with it. Trust yourself and the process.

Create a system of support for yourself. Although I am your mother, your confidant, and biggest cheerleader, you need a network outside of the home to support you through this journey called life. Be sure to have an eclectic group of people in your corner, both men and women. As you fully develop into manhood, seek those who may serve as a friend, mentor, counselor, spiritual guide, professional consultant, financial guru... Make sure these individuals are able to impart wisdom and that the qualities these supporting cast members possess reassemble the characteristics that were instilled in you from the beginning. Your supporting cast may change through time and will prove to be valuable at various phases throughout your life.

In every situation remember to trust the process. God will always make a way, no matter what. Understand the pulse of your mental health and make adjustments as needed along the way.

Love,

Mom

Your Mental Health is the heartbeat of your life YOU are important!

By Lisa Millner-Little

In our community, the word therapist is frowned upon terribly and carries a stigma that you are "crazy". Our beliefs have always been just attending church and let the pastors pray for you. If you are praying hard enough things will be fine, you will snap out of it! When that doesn't happen, we feel like God has abandoned us. This lack of knowledge leads many to believe that a mental health condition is a personal weakness or some sort of punishment from God. Sometimes our community may be reluctant to discuss mental health issues and seek treatment because of the shame and stigma associated with such conditions. I do believe in this method (church) as well, but where the root of that method came from was the church was the only place our forefathers found refuge because they did not have the accessibility to doctors. All they had was their faith in God. But as generations progressed we produced doctors, lawyers, journalists, writers, and yes therapists.

Life is full of adventures and trials. As you grow through the phases of being your God-ordained authentic self you will understand that it is not things that matter the most in life but having peace of mind is priceless. Many young men have not been told how to process and talk about their emotional experiences, which furthers a sense of isolation, anger, and resentment. This creates emotional volatility that can sometimes manifest in seeming "shut down" in relationships and friendships. At its worst, this budding resentment can manifest in an outward expression of anger, aggression, and even violence.

Many young men (arguably most) struggle with the idea of being openly vulnerable and sharing their emotions. And for those who grew up as sensitive boys, they are often subject to ridicule and shaming for what are natural and healthy expressions of emotion. Black boys face a unique challenge in that most of what is most prized about them may be their looks or bodies, but rarely ever their intellect and emotional intelligence. These things are often deemed too soft for any Black man to experience, delivering the message that if you are those things then you must change...and fast.

In reviewing the alarming statistics, I found the category of leading causes of death, when broken down by age group for black males in the U.S., was disturbing. For young black men between the ages of 15 and 34, the number one cause of death in 2016 was a homicide. A report from the U.S. Surgeon General found that from 1980 - 1995, the suicide rate among African Americans ages 10 to 14 increased 233 percent, as compared to 120 percent of non-Hispanic whites. So, why is this? Experts agree that it is likely to be a combination of factors, from society's expectation of 'men' to a desire to solve one's own problems.

I'm intentionally listing this alarming information to bring a heightened awareness that YOU matter. If there comes a time in life where you feel ongoing rejection, anxiety, racism, unwantedness, overlooked, and depressed to name a few. You need to talk about it! Silence and stoicism – denying oneself help in order to appear strong – need to be overcome. True strength lies in recognizing the need for help and seeking it out. Understanding that you are not the first to experience these emotions and not suppressing these feelings can and ultimately lead to a healthy life. You can then notice patterns of behaviors, lessons on what to avoid, what to embrace, how to detox your very soul to have a long and fulfilling life.

Our desire as a parent for you to go to school if you want to gain higher education prepares now, if not you need a viable trade. It's not just about the money but it has been proven that individuals of lower economic status, have stressors that can accompany poverty – hunger, homelessness, lack of other basic needs or an inability to find jobs or afford treatment – can be contributing factors that lead to mental health issues. Our sons are more likely than other children to be exposed to violence, which can have a profound, long-term effect on their mental health. The risk of developing a mental health condition such as post-traumatic stress disorder, depression, and anxiety Without proper treatment, mental health conditions can worsen and make day-to-day life harder.

One of the most integral components in your mind. Your mental health is inseparable from your physical health. My desire is for you to look like what is on the inside of you, whole, healthy, and complete. It's okay to feel depressed. It's okay to feel overwhelmed. It's okay to be sad. It's okay to be anxious. It's okay to be scared. It's okay to not have everything figured out, to feel a wave of uncertainty come crashing over you and not know which way is up, or when your next gulp of air will come. These are perfectly normal feelings that every man experiences. And it's okay to talk about it. What's not okay is suffering in silence.

I want you to know that it is okay to ask for HELP! Even if it is not me, seek counseling, involve yourself with people who are open-minded and positive. With the conditions of society today it seems as if we are going back in time and there is a repeat of the 1960s. But this time we are stronger, better, and wiser. You can change the world. You are what God wanted in the earth realm now. Fully equipped to conquer every adversary that comes to hinder, delay, or destroy the LIFE that was given as a gift. Don't get me wrong, suffering is a part of the process, but tools are made available that you maintain your true authentic self through life's ups and downs. You can be all that you have envisioned. It will take dedication and hard work on your behalf. This means on the days you feel heavy, overwhelmed of course affirm yourself through prayer, declarations but if it persists make an appointment.

I want you to understand that getting help is what makes you strong. Strength sometimes comes to us in the form of disclosure of a wounded area in our life. Just like when you fell as a child, I only allowed you to keep the band-aid over your scar for a couple of days because I knew it needed exposure to heal. So, it shall be when you feel emotionally stressed or strained. Seek professional help, it is not a curse. I have intentionally committed myself to self-care to be that example for you. It may look different for each season of your life, but you are so important that it is necessary. It could be taking a day off work, eating better, exercise to release tension, being open with me, or another understanding family member about where you are. I am committed to being a safe place for you, there's no shaming, there's no blaming, and there's no cutting off the conversation. It's just a safe space. YOU are important and your mental health is the heartbeat of your life.

You will come to understand that life is full of ups and downs everyone has them, but it is how you process through yours and get the lesson and move on. There is no official blueprint in life that says if you do this then this will happen...oh no, you can honestly do everything right and out of the blue something totally unexpected can occur and change your entire being. So, you must always take care of YOU! Before an airplane takes off, the flight attendant goes over the safety precautions and they ask you to apply your mask first and then assist others. I think this will be crucial in your life as well, be healed then heal. Sometimes we forget about our own importance and it is so easy to do with the tidal waves of life coming upon the people you love and care for. "But to thine own self always be true"!

I want you to keep in your mind on those days when life is peaking, blessing, and glorious to make sure you enjoy, bask, and relish those moments in time. These memories will prove to be beneficial on those days that seem bottomless, hopeless they will make your heartbeat again. One of my favorite passages is found in Philippians 4:8 and it says Finally, brethren, whatever things are true, whatever things are noble, whatever things are just, whatever things are pure, whatever things are lovely, whatever things are of good report if there is any virtue and if there is anything praiseworthy—meditate on these things. Meditation is just you sitting quietly with your eyes closed, taking a few deep breaths in and out and relaxing. Begin to then be intentional with your thoughts…positive only. I like to put on worship music or even acoustic sounds to help me relax and get in the mode where I can release all tension and stress. It Is like a reset button to recharge for the next day, hour, or even minute. Meditation allows you to take inventory of your own body to decompress so you can increase your mental clarity and focus.

I so wish someone had sat me down in my earlier years and taught me this. I think I could have compartmentalized some things differently and the impact would not have been so traumatic.

The good news is…I'm telling you and this is one generational cycle that can and will be broken off my legacy. We are not always going to be able to hide; push things aside and never deal with them. YOU are so important to me that I want you to learn now how to process through pain but more importantly come out healed and wiser for it. Life is a journey! Enjoy and always take care of YOU!

YOU are important to ME!

Love,

Moma

Your Steps for Success

By D. JaMese Morris Black

"A solid foundation builds solid success" We have strived to give you the needed tools to build your foundation as a man. We have taught you the importance of God, Family, and Finances. Many times in our teaching, we have shown you what you should NOT do versus what to do. Those lessons are just as important as the "what you should do" lessons. In everything you do, every step you make, every thought you have, God must be included. He will be your voice of reason and discernment. There will be many weapons formed against you, but with God's guidance and support, they will not prosper. Live with all of your actions reflexing a touch of God, you will be successful.

"Relax and be" Do not allow your life goals to prevent you from just living and enjoying life. Ecclesiastes 3: 1-13 reminds us there is a time (season) for everything in our lives. Many of your ancestors passed through this land with one focus. Work. Yes, that is a key factor in life! Also, taking a moment to just breathe can help with extending your time on earth. Happiness can bring a sense of peace that nothing can remove. Life will force you to work hard and pour negative feelings and ideas into your spirit. Walking away and reviving your mind is an unchangeable factor.

"It is on a Wheel" Your grandfather, Rev. James Robert Morris, instilled in me a key factor that you need to take and manifest your actions also.. Be very careful how you treat others. Just as your actions are like the wheels on a car, what goes around comes around. What you put into the atmosphere will come back to you. You often asked me why did I always stop and help older women? Well, I believed that my actions would transfer to my mother. Someone would stop and help her when she needed it. Sometimes others pay for your choices - good or bad.

As you walk your steps, people will always remember how you treated them, not what you said to them.

"Be your own "Jones" There is a common saying in life, " Keeping up with the Joneses" what that means son, many people strive to emulate the lives of others. Many times causing unnecessary stress and hardship to you. The harsh reality is when life is spent trying to copy the life of others, many do not see the struggle of the "Jones". Son, strive to be the best you can be and create your own life and lifestyle that brings you happiness and peace. So what, if your car is not the top of the line! A car depreciates every time you crank it. But, you will have additional funds to travel and enjoy new experiences. Yes, there will be others who will question your choices of material gain, but as I have tried to instill into you, their questions do not matter unless there is a check of support from them with their questions.

"Speak Life into a Dead Situation" Make a difference in every environment you walk into. Do not live this life focused on just you and what you can only gain. There will be times when you will find yourself needing to alter a situation or environment. Find the strength to do it. Leave any space better than you found it.

Are You Living A Balanced Life?

By Shanta Y. Jackson

Son,

I see you watching what you eat, working out constantly, and drinking your water. I love it. I love the commitment you have made to be physically fit. You are an inspiration! You go after what you love, and you commit to it. After playing football in middle school and seeing you yearn to be called from the sidelines, you made the necessary changes to get called first. You are already learning how to make the changes necessary to achieve your goals. You have had to balance schoolwork, a job and still making enough time to keep your room clean all while staying physically fit. And, these are key lessons to living a balanced life.

No matter where you are in life, balance will be key. You can't be so focused on one thing that all the other things fall apart. For example, let's say that you have been working out constantly but you failed to study your academic class work. What will likely happen? You will not have the grades to play on the field and miss game night. Another example would be you studying your heart out and working out but neglecting to clean your room. You can get out on the field and play but getting to the game and organizing all the equipment you need slows you down and makes a huge impact on your state of mind. So, instead of being mentally prepared for the game, you are still trying to calm down from your desperate search a few hours earlier when you couldn't find one of your socks, shoes, or mouthguard. You see, balance is a balancing act.

Now, here is the interesting part. If you learn how to balance key elements in your life now, it will be easier twenty years from now.

But, what does a balanced life look like? Well, I personally believe it includes physical wellness (eating to live and moving to gain strength), spiritual wellness (a belief in something greater than yourself), mental wellness (the ability to feel why things are going on in your life and finding solutions that move you forward) and financial wellness (the art of valuing money for what it is, just a conduit to living a fruitful and meaningful life filled with purpose).

And, yes, you read that right! Financial wellness is included. For so many years, in our family, money wasn't something we talked about. We knew we needed money to survive but we didn't talk about what we did when we received the money. This followed me into my adult life and let me tell you, not learning the value of money can hurt. **A lot.** I lost and wasted a lot of money simply because I didn't have a plan for it. I made money and even saved a little but for the most part, money was a necessary evil and not a tool to use to create the life I wanted.

And, the sad reality is, that the constant need for money slowly destroyed the balance I needed to make powerful moves. I mean, I wasted years of my life. The constant worry, fear and, just plain sleepless nights that came from a lack of money took over my life. I didn't work out enough, eat the right foods and, failed to make my faith and connection to God a priority. I was walking with fear every day like it was a companion.

And, then something happened. I realized something powerful. Whenever I was pregnant with either you or Adric, I was in my stride. I ate well, exercised and planned everything to a "T". And, after I had you or your brother, I fell back into my old routines. What happened? I realized that I did all those things so that you all would have a great start to life. I loved you with every inch of my being before I could even see you. And, after I had you two, I went back to who I was. My epiphany was that I needed to love myself as much as I loved each of you. You see when you truly love yourself, you do the necessary things to be fruitful and purposeful.

Loving yourself and financial wellness are not often talked about in the same circles, but I believe when you connect the dots, you will gain insight and be able to truly live a great life.

There are four principles that I believe can give you the purpose of your money. Those four principles are:

(1) Budgeting to live and grow
(2) Developing your saving muscle
(3) Know your numbers
(4) Make ownership "king" in your life.

Son, you can start today with your financial wellness by budgeting every time you receive money. You are so blessed to have grandparents and aunties that think enough of you to give you money. The next time you receive money, sit down and plan for that money. Assign your money to a task. Use a book and write out that plan. You can assign a portion of your money towards going out, gas for the car and clothes. The thing to remember is that if you don't assign your money a task, it can be used up with no purpose. And, you will be feeling dismayed that your money is gone, and you can't retrace your footsteps to see where the money went. Practice this. Make this a habit. If you master budgeting now, you will be able to create the life you want.

While you are budgeting, assign part of your money to save. Now, I was always told to pay yourself first, but I never truly knew what that meant. So, I am going to tell you what I was told by a great Certified Public Account (CPA) . A CPA is a trusted financial advisor so their whole world is about numbers and money. So, when a CPA gives you advice, you take it. Before you pay any bills, put a percentage towards your savings. That means before you go out to eat, or go to the movies or buy any new tech gadget, put money aside in a separate account to go toward you and your future. And, that's it. It seems simple, but this little step will build your wealth.

I want you to practice saving every chance you get. Just like building muscle means doing repetitions repeatedly, that is the same with saving. When you are building muscle, you start with the smaller weights and once your body has mastered that weight, you go to the heavier weights. Likewise, start off small while saving, and once that gets easy, start increasing the amounts. Build that savings muscle!!

I know you love seeing your money grow in your account, and I secretly smile, because I know that you will be a millionaire one day with your work ethic. However, although saving your money is great, as you get older, you will be responsible for more things. You will have to pay your car insurance, car note, internet bill and more. As you are assigning your money, make sure you are paying your debts on time. By constantly paying your bills on time, you will be increasing your credit score. A credit score is basically a written record of debt repayment. The more you pay your debts on time or as agreed, the higher your credit score will be. Scores range from 300 to over 800. Any credit score above 640 is considered good and any credit score above 700 is considered great. While a credit score is not an indication of the type of person you are in life, it is used to determine whether you can rent an apartment, buy a house or even get a job. Knowing your numbers will help you know where you are. Knowing your numbers will mean that you can make decisions about big purchases. Knowing your numbers will mean that you will know what to rebuild and what to let go. Knowing your numbers keeps you in control! And being in control is so much better than letting your finances be in control of you.

Once credit is not an obstacle, the world is your oyster. I mean it. You will be able to plan a real future for yourself. Man, I wish I learned this lesson from the beginning. It has taken me over three decades to learn this one fact. But, it doesn't stop there. Whatever you do, make sure you own it. Want a car, don't lease it, buy it. Want to find somewhere to live, don't rent a home, buy one. Working and developing skills from a job, at some point, start your own business. Ownership expands your revenue stream and has more advantages. Never be afraid to own anything. Yes, it will be more responsibility, more paperwork but don't let anything get in your way. Owning your skills, owning your vehicles, owning the buildings where you work, will allow that control I talked about earlier. Ownership is "KING."

And, Son, you are a King. A King is able to look over his life and make it his own. Living a balanced life helps you create, live abundantly and dream. Learn to keep your mind steady by strengthening your relationship with God, increasing your physical strength for endurance, while keeping your mental endurance strong and by learning to keep your finances in control. Money is nothing to run away from. It is a tool to leap forward. Remember to budget for your priorities, save with the future in mind, pay your bills on-time, know your credit score and let being an owner guide your steps. Your future is bright and I can see it so clearly.

Sex and Responsibility

By Juandalynn Jones-Hunt

Dear son,

It is with great care and concern that I feel compiled to discuss with you the responsibilities that accompany the act of sex and the decision to participate in such. There is a responsibility to self, to others, and to your livelihood. The consequences linked to the act of sex require commitment, compromise, and dedication. It would behoove anyone with an interest, in the act, to be clear and deliberate in their decision to move forward. One must be clear regarding the understanding of the possible outcomes of having sex. One must also be deliberate in precautionary measures to protect themselves, to protect others, and to prevent procreation where the end result isn't advantageous.

I say all of that to say, "Boy! Don't be a fool!"

I don't care how much you think that rubber is in the way. That's its job. To be in the way. It needs to be in the way of herpes, HIV/AIDS, chlamydia, gonorrhea, and more. There are diseases that you could catch that may basically leave your "junk" looking like ground beef. And that's if you are lucky. AIDS could write your death sentence for you. The choice to wear a condom is a responsible one for the protection of self and others.

If a lifelong illness or death by a STD isn't scary enough, think of this. You are depositing bits of yourself into others. You are a king. Who then is worthy enough of being she who shall carry with her any of you? Be wise in your choices, son. Be mindful that your seed is your legacy. Who shall you be bound to you for a lifetime? Look around you. You hear your boys crying about these "chickenheads" keeping them in court whittling their paychecks down to the nub and they don't even know if the money is going to their kids. They are left struggling to get ahead because they are now paying for about 20 minutes of "head". And paying the price for a minimum of 18 years to a woman they don't even like anymore, who is also the mother of their own offspring. That is a major role to hand to an understudy. They should have been more careful, as the responsibility of raising a child is both that of the mother and the father, regardless of how feelings change up. Easy "tail" ain't such an easy trail to be bound to for a lifetime. I beg of you to choose wisely, son. If you can't bring her home to properly meet your folks, then "how you gon' present" her as the mother of your future prince or princess?

Might I suggest that love be the premise for selecting whom you would even consider having sex. Love doesn't fail. Love can withstand pressures and overcome obstacles. Love will be by your side on this journey. Love begets loves and love gives love freely. Love ushers in peace, tranquility and happiness. Love is not accompanied with strife and chaos. Love is that which you should seek. The act of sex is precious to those who first have love. Sex for any other reason is a wasted opportunity to gain access to she who was truly meant for you. It eliminates your chance of finding "your queen".

Know your purpose and your worth. Be wise in your decisions, my love. Be wise, for your wellness, happiness, and livelihood rest upon the decision of having sex or not.

With all my dearest concern for you,
Mom

It's Okay

By Audrey Abrams

When you were conceived a spiritual celebration began in my belly and it completely took over my soul. You are two of the greatest loves I have ever known and some of the most precious gifts I have ever been given. When I tell you that you are ok, it is because my faith in you is bigger than you will ever know.

It is ok to be one hundred percent you, so go ahead and perform to the music in your head, even if it's not the music your friends hear, even if it's not the music you were told to hear. So many times, we get caught up in our peers' lives and being a part of their surroundings that we forget to be ourselves. I want you to always be you, even when it hurts. You choosing to march to your own beat proves your strength and defines the true inner you.

It is ok you both made some decisions you thought I would never forgive you for. Some of those decisions turned out to be a few of my better blessings, one is currently 11 and the other 9. Cj never did you let being a young dad slow you down, you kept pushing for your goal of college and you reached it. Even as you were taking your last breath you were in the midst of your dreams and for that, I am extremely proud of you.

It is ok that you spent your 16th birthday in juvenile detention center John, you did not allow that mistake to define you as a man, you took the blemish and made it a coma, you paid the price and you grew wiser. You wrote a startup business plan and figured out how to finance it, and for that I say I am extremely proud of you. Your dedication to stepping up to fill some of your brother's responsibilities that he left behind does not go unnoticed, and if none ever acknowledges it just know it's ok because it is exactly what you are supposed to do.

It is ok to be sensitive; sensitivity is not a quality of a weak man but of a man that knows who he is regardless of what society says he should be. Your sensitive side is what allowed you to be a nourishing father Cj and John you a fantastic uncle, keep that quality. Often I saw you cry, keep crying, it cleanses your mind and your heart allowing new growth and the strength you need to fix your crown and finish your race.

It's ok to love, often men treat love as a noun, love is an action word requiring the use of all senses, use it as such. If you ever feel love becoming a noun it's time to evaluate who you are loving. Also remember that your ego is not a characteristic of love, ego is a self-centered quality that has no business in the same room as love. Men are often taught to allow their egos to get in the way of showing someone how they really feel about them, so allow love to consume all of you, never expecting nothing in return. When you start expecting a return on your investment you are no longer in love, you have loved and lost.

Its ok to have weird feelings that you don't quite understand from time to time, those feelings may appear in the form of anxiety, depression or even simple anger, but the key is to not let those unexplainable feelings get the best of you, any feeling you have is real and should be shared so it can be understood.

It is ok that your route to manhood was somewhat a hurricane instead of an adventure, I'm sure your survival has taught you that no storm is proven too much for God.

It's ok for you to know that I am not perfect, I mess up just like you, the difference is as adults we can hide our mess ups better than children. Know that if I messed up with you and on you, but it was my head and not my heart. My heart will always be pure for you and I need you to be ok with that, understanding that.

It is ok Cj that you left your siblings to deal with your death, it made them resilient, and their bond now is something that I don't even try to understand.

It's ok that you left me, even when I wasn't ready to let you go. Truth is the hardest thing I've done in life was to bury you, but it was preparation for what I would do next. God's grace carries me every day.

Lastly CJ,I want you to know it's ok leaving us in charge of watering your flowers, we will love them just as hard as we loved you. We will share your memories with them every chance we get, and they will know that you were a dad that loved them more than you loved yourself. We will remind them that even though we loved you, God loved you best, and your absence makes us stronger than ever because living without you is not for the weak at heart.

About the

Authors

Ocir JaRon Black

Ocir JaRon Black is the son of Marquis RonRico "Rico" Black and D. JaMese Morris Black . He is the oldest of two. Ocir along with his twin brother Zyon JaRiq Black was born in Florence, South Carolina and lives in Winston-Salem, North Carolina.

"O" as many call him, is currently a sophomore at the Early College of Forsyth, in Winston-Salem, North Carolina. He is also a student athlete who runs track for Parkland High School. His career goals include becoming a Lawyer, as well as, an entrepreneur. He excels in reading, writing and above all activism. He is rooted and promotes strong family values and strives to gain a deep understanding of his history and culture.

The concept of this book was close to his heart as it displays the relationship between Mothers and Sons. This was a special bond that was established with his grandmothers and mother. The goal for all who read is to gain an understanding of how mothers feel and believe when it comes to raising their sons. Also, his vision is to provide guidance and support to those struggling to understand a mother's view and love that exists for their growing and in some cases grown black males.

D. JaMese Morris Black

D. JaMese Morris Black was born to Rev. James R. and Sallie M. Morris (Redd) both have crossed into eternity. JaMese was reared in Henry County, Virginia, and is the youngest of three- Derrick JaSal Morris and Rev. DaRon JeSie Morris hold the title of her brothers.

In the Summer of 1999, Morris was united in holy matrimony to Marquis RonRico "Rico" Black. God has blessed this union with their amazing twin boys: Ocir JaRon and Zyon JaRiq.

Black holds a Master's degree in Educational Leadership and a Bachelor of Arts degree in History and English from High Point University.

D. JaMese M. Black's career in education began at Rockingham County High School, Wentworth, NC in 1998, where she was a social studies teacher. She served as a social studies teacher for seven years prior to becoming Curriculum Facilitator at Weaver Academy and Early/Middle College at Bennett in Greensboro, North Carolina, a position she held for four years. She was Assistant Principal of Instruction at Bartlett Yancey High School in Yanceyville, North Carolina from 2008-2009 and at Northeast Guilford High School in McLeansville, North Carolina from 2011-2014. She became the principal of Magna Vista High School in Ridgeway, Virginia in 2014. She transformed the school to become accredited within one year. She led Magna Vista until 2017 upon her decision to step down to care for her mother.

She returned to administration as Principal of East Montgomery High School in Biscoe, NC in 2018. She is the 2019-20 Principal of the Year for Montgomery County Schools. This was given after her first year in the district and turning around her school within the year to make growth. She is the Executive Director of Instructional Innovation and Student Support.

LaShonda Scott Douglas

LaShonda Scott Douglas has worked within the educational field in many different capacities. From beginning as a substitute teacher, to embarking upon graduating with her Bachelor of Arts, in Educational Studies. Contributing author of, **Love Letter To My Son**, has brought together the relationship with our sons during such a time as this. Words and their true meanings have always been intriguing to me.

There's no difference in how we choose to speak to our sons, to either build them up, or break them down. My love and dedication to God as a servant, mother and writer drives me to look for every opportunity to be that encouragement or smile for one that may simply need it. Sometimes the smallest, most insignificant moments in our lives, are the most life changing to someone else. Be that change.

T.C. Evans

T. C. EVANS, a graduate of Winston-Salem State University with a Bachelor of Science and Walden University with a Masters in Public Administration. Her career started as an Occupational Therapist with a current emphasis in Pediatric Therapy. She is the proud parent of one son, Bryson. In her free time, she finds interests in women's basketball, general sports, music, creating projects, writing, and youth outreach. She currently resides in Durham, North Carolina.

Shanta Y. Jackson

Shanta Jackson is a business owner, mentor, and real estate agent in the Raleigh/Durham North Carolina area. Shanta has helped hundreds of families find home buying success by compassionately advising them along the path towards smart homeownership. Shanta not only stays abreast of the most current trends in the real estate industry, but she keeps a close watch on government policies ensuring that she is able to guide her clients through tough decisions in an ever-changing market. She is the managing broker of her company, Jackson Realty Group, and has been featured in an episode along with her client in HGTV's House Hunters.

While Shanta has spent several years growing and nurturing her business, nothing compares to the roles that have shaped how she sees the world today. Being the wife, to her business partner, Victor Jackson and mom to her sons, Amir, aged 16 and Adric aged 4, has been the most important role in her life.

Guided by her strong faith in God and sound belief in her family, Shanta plans to take on each new journey with vigor and enthusiasm.

Juandalynn JaCinta Jones-Hunt

Juandalynn JaCinta Jones-Hunt is the daughter of Mr. Lawrence E. Jones & Mrs. Lula B. (Hairston) Jones of Henry County, VA. She has achieved National Boards for Professional Teachers certification twice, in the area of Visual Arts for adolescent to young adults. Juandalynn currently holds teaching certificates in the state of North Carolina and the Commonwealth of Virginia. She is currently a visual arts educator at Parkview Village Elementary Expressive Arts Magnet School, where she was selected the teacher of the year for 2015-16 and has served as the team leader and as a mentor. The George Washington Carver High School (Fieldale, VA) graduate also holds the following degrees: a Post Baccalaureate Certificate from the University of North Carolina-Greensboro in Women's & Genders Studies; a Bachelor of Arts in Studio Arts, a Bachelor of Science in Art Education, a Masters in English Literature Education from the University of NC- Pembroke. Juandalynn is currently a doctoral degree candidate at Northcentral University for Teaching and Curriculum. She is a member of Delta Sigma Theta, Inc. and several other professional and community service organizations.

She has served as the Primary Director for the Guilford County Association of Educator and as a state delegate for the organization. During the summer of 2019, she served in an administrative position in one of the largest arts and academic enrichment camps in the state of N.C., Ignite Camp and was the curriculum director for UNCG's award winning All-Arts & Sciences Camp. Juandalynn is a member of the NCAE Instructional Leaders Institute. She has been selected to participate in several national summer teacher institutes. Jones-Hunt has served as a member of the AdvanceED national school accreditation team. In 2015, Jones-Hunt was recognized, in a weekly online newsletter, by the White House Initiative on Educational Excellence for African Americans. Her past honors include being a graduate research presenter at a national conference at Sarah Lawrence College in New York, repeat presenter at the No Child Left Behind/Closing the Gap Conferences in the state of North Carolina, High Point's Outstanding Young Educator of the Year, Communities in Schools Teacher of the Year, writer of several educational grants, and induction to Greensboro's 40 Leaders Under Forty award. Jones-Hunt was named Fox 8 New NC Lottery Educator of the Week (January 2020).

She is the widow of Bruce W. Hunt, mother of Greensboro Police Officer Kai Christian Hunt, and sister of the late Officer Ephraim S. Jones. She has a granddaughter, Kaila Daenerys of Salisbury, NC. She resides in Greensboro, NC.

Catina M. King

Catina Marcella King was born in Martinsville, Virginia to Phyllis Jean Clack (Spencer) and James Morris Clack. Both of her parents are deceased and resting in the arms of God. She has one sister, Stacey D. Clack, and three brothers, Wanzo D. Clack, James Pritchett, and Marcus Pritchett. Catina accepted Jesus Christ as her Lord and Savior at a young age; however, through life challenges strayed away. She re-dedicated her life to Christ in 1997 and has lived according to God's teaching since that time. She joined Crossover Fellowship Church (Now Friends Family Worship Center) in 2009. While being an active member of the ministry, she serves on the Hospitality Team, Women's Ministry, and Pastor's Aide Committee.

Catina' s relationship with Christ is sacred and very important to her. When she re-dedicated her life to God, she asked God to keep His hands on her life and guide every area of her life. She has always been very specific with God, so with that, she picked up this saying "One Day Lord". Those close to her would laugh every time she would say it until they saw the hand of God working. Catina's "One Day Lord" came September 26, 2015, when she was united in holy matrimony to her "King" Christopher Conrad King. She also gained a son Christian King, her husband's oldest child. God later blessed this union with an amazing Son Christoff Josiah King on April 27, 2017. In addition, Catina and Christopher share the joy of having a granddaughter, whom they love very much. Because family is very important to Catina, she embraces every moment she has with her family.

Catina has worked in the Mental Health profession since 1993. She began her journey working with the developmentally disabled population from 1993-1997. She was then offered an opportunity to work with At-Risk teens and has continued working with this population from 1997 to Present. Catina is currently a Program Coordinator and she wears many hats in this position. She has enjoyed every challenge and accomplishment that follows while in this career. She is also very dependable, insightful and a patient person. Catina has skills and training that enables her to process and de-escalate intense situations. These qualities allow her to assess each situation and make decisions that would better serve or benefit everyone she meets.

One of Catina's Favorite scripture that helps keep her grounded is Proverbs 21:21 He that followeth after righteousness and mercy findeth life, righteousness, and honour

About the Authors

Audrey Abrams Lee

Audrey Abrams Lee was born Audrey Denise Abrams, the third child of Margaret Redfearn Abrams and John Ecker Abrams. Audrey grew up in Thomasville and is a graduate of Thomasville High School in 1986 and High Point University in 2005.

Audrey is one of four children, she has two sisters Yvette and Kristi and one brother, John.

Audrey gave birth to three children, Britteny, who is currently 33, John, who is currently 27 and Quinton Jr. who crossed over in March of 2013 at the age of 21. Audrey is Mimi to six grandchildren that range in age from three to eleven.

Audrey is currently married to James Lee Jr. from Rural Hall NC and resides in Kernersville. Audrey is the owner of Ca-Doodles Childcare in Thomasville NC and loves to travel and spend time with friends and family.

Audrey has worked in the area of medical insurance, has taught high school and has been involved with mentoring young women.

Lisa Millner-Little

Lisa Little is a native of Martinsville VA, where she was born and raised. The eldest child of Pastors Henry and Arnita Davis – Mt. Zion AME Church in Greensboro, NC, a preacher's kid (PK). She is one who is passionate about her faith and her family. Lisa has two great accomplishments to date, her sons Jeron, Senior at Winston-Salem State University and, Justin, a recent graduate of NC A&T Middle College. Lisa is also the devoted wife of Ray Little. The apple does not fall too far from the tree, she has been an ordained Elder in the Lord's Church since 2013. A firm believer that pain reveals power and despair propels you to your destiny. Lisa is anointed, vibrant, powerful, and longs to empower others in their God-given attributes.

Currently, she is employed by the United States Postal Service as a Human Resource Personnel Specialist. Although Lisa is a strong enthusiastic communicator and motivator her true character is one who is warm-hearted and down to earth working hard to impart and empower hope to everyone who crosses her path that is ready to go after their destiny! The motto that she has based her life on can be found in the scriptures: Romans 8:18 which states, "For I reckon that the sufferings of this present time are not worthy to be compared with the glory which shall be revealed in us" and in her!

Ruthmarie B. Mitchell

Ruthmarie Mitchell has worked for Guilford County Schools for the past 21 years. She began her educational career in 1999 at Northeast Guilford High School, in McLeansville, NC. Over the course of the next 14 years, Ms. Mitchell would serve as a Spanish teacher, school counselor, graduation coach, and assistant principal. In the fall of 2013, Ms. Mitchell transferred to Smith High School as an assistant principal and in the fall of 2015, transferred to David D. Jones Elementary. This fall (2020), Ms. Mitchell will join Colfax Elementary School as their assistant principal.

Ms. Mitchell participated in the Aspiring Leadership Development Program in 2015-16 and is also a selected member of the GCS Equity Leadership Development Program. As an equity leader, Ms. Mitchell has provided school-wide professional development on topics focused on Equity, Tolerance, Diversity, Racism, and other inequities.

Ms. Mitchell is an only child originally from New York. Ms. Mitchell has lived in various places, both stateside and abroad. A great deal of her childhood and young adult years were spent in Tucson, AZ. She has two children, two bonus sons, and six beautiful granddaughters. Ms. Mitchell holds a Bachelor's Degree in Romance Languages and Lit (French and Spanish for K-12) from North Carolina Agricultural & Technical State University., a Master's Degree in Counseling Education from North Carolina A&T State University, and a Master's Degree in School Administration from the University of North Carolina at Greensboro.

Having worked in Title I schools and directly with a diverse student population as a classroom teacher, counselor, graduation coach, and administrator, she brings a unique perspective that creates a successful partnership between administrators, teachers, parents, and most importantly, students. She feels grateful to partner with incredible people who believe in helping every child succeed academically, socially, and emotionally. She believes this is non-negotiable if your calling is education.

One of the key components of her educational philosophy is that she believes ALL children have the capacity to learn and grow every single year, regardless of their circumstances. The key is to develop, nurture, build relationships and create trust with each individual student and their caregivers. After that, the sky's the limit!

Sondra Trice-Jones

Sondra's life began in 1965; she was born to Charles and Beatrice Trice on March 13, 1965 at St. John's Episcopal Hospital in New York City. She was raised in Bedford - Stuyvesant Brooklyn, NY. Sondra was the younger of two girls. When her family moved to Durham, NC in 1979 without her big sister, she was left feeling like an only child. She graduated from Durham High School in 1983 and went off to attend UNC- Greensboro. She left college and pursued Cosmetology in 1985. After receiving her Cosmetologist license, Sondra opened her first hair salon- Salon 323 in downtown Durham. She serviced the hair industry for approximately fifteen years, retiring in 1997 to raise her son. She married his father in 2001 the year of 911 and they were divorced in 2004.

In 2002, she opened her first adolescent group home for boys and was in the Mental Health Industry for over ten years. Sondra held the position of President for two Non-Profit Organizations- Women in Action for the Prevention of Violence and its Causes and Women4Women, Inc. and Vice-President of Journey's Home, LLC and Journey's Community Partners, Inc. In 2012 she enrolled in Real Estate school. Sondra hung her license at Keller Williams for two years and decided to open up her own firm; she named it Ultra Realty.

She is now the Broker-In-Charge of a very successful business with her own team. She is happily married and in her spare time, she loves to travel and shop as well as being a wife, mom and a grandmother. She just celebrated her 55th birthday and she still feels that the sky's the limit.

Tomeka W. Wormack

Tomeka A. Wormack is the daughter of Mr. and Mrs. Charles Wilson Allen, Jr. She was born and raised in Wilmington, NC. She was later transplanted in Winston-Salem, NC in 1993 and graduated with a Bachelor's degree in nursing in 1997 from Winston-Salem State University. During her college career, she was active in the nursing sorority, Chi Eta Phi Sorority, Incorporated and dance groups.

After working many years as a floor nurse, she decided to further advance her nursing career. Tomeka went back to her Alma Mater to obtain her Master's degree in 2004 as a Family Nurse Practitioner and also happened to be part of that first graduating class for the program. She has been working in the Preoperative Assessment Clinic (PAC) at Wake Forest Baptist Hospital for the last 16 years, aside from the additional six years in other departments with that same company.

Tomeka is married to Jimmy Wormack, Jr, who is also a Winston-Salem State University Alumni. They enjoy the journey of raising their 13-year-old son, Jimmy Allen Wormack. She is also a part of the illustrious organization, Delta Sigma Theta Sorority, Incorporated where she is active and participates in community service. She has two older sisters, Abigail Bingham and Panza Mcneill, who are also her Sorors.

In her spare time, Tomeka enjoys dancing, exercising, spending time with her family and friends, and watching her son play sports. Let's not forget to mention her interesting shoe addiction. The one thing that she really enjoys most is encouraging others, whether it be a family member, friend, her patients, or even a stranger in need of a listening ear. The one thing she always wants people to take away from their encounter with her is that " There's nothing you and God can't handle together but you have to let Him lead".

Made in the USA
Monee, IL
27 February 2021